Backward children

Arthur Holmes

Alpha Editions

This edition published in 2019

ISBN : 9789353862978

Design and Setting By
Alpha Editions
email - alphaedis@gmail.com

BACKWARD CHILDREN

By

ARTHUR HOLMES

Dean of the General Faculty of the Pennsylvania
State College and Author of The
Conservation of the Child

CHILDHOOD AND YOUTH SERIES

EDITED BY M. V. O'SHEA

Professor of Education, The University of Wisconsin

INDIANAPOLIS
THE BOBBS-MERRILL COMPANY
PUBLISHERS

TO MY WIFE

WHOSE QUIET DEVOTION TO STUDY
UNDER DIFFICULTIES HAS SO MANY TIMES
INSPIRED MY FALTERING
DILIGENCE

EDITOR'S INTRODUCTION

We are these days reading and hearing a good deal about backward children. When is a child backward? May he be backward in some ways and forward in others? Are children backward by birth, or are they made so by neglect or bad methods of training? What are the signs of backwardness? Is there any way of determining accurately whether or not a given child is permanently arrested? Could the parent and the teacher help an unfortunate child if they could early detect his shortcomings? What part do physical causes play in mental and moral backwardness? Is retardation in childhood and youth ever due to the use of stimulants such as tea, coffee, cocoa and alcoholic beverages? What part does food play in determining whether or not a child will be normal intellectually and morally?

These questions and others like them are of supreme importance to-day to teachers and parents. People are seeking light from every source on the problems of the backward child. It is the purpose of this volume to discuss all these matters in a scientific but at the same time simple, concrete and practical way. The author, Dean Holmes, has had unusual opportunities to study the subject of backwardness in its various aspects, theoretical and practical. He is one of the very small number of persons in this country who have dealt with the subnormal child in the laboratory and the clinic as well as in the home and the school. He has given us new conceptions of what backwardness means, and especially of its varieties, its causes, and practical remedies therefor in home and school.

There is not much literature available in English on the subject of backward children, and even the few books and articles that are accessible deal with the subject in a rather general way. Dean Holmes, however, as the title of his volume indicates, treats concrete cases of backwardness. He pictures vividly the typical varieties of children who give parents and teachers trouble. He goes into sufficient detail so that the type can be easily recognized. Instead of discussing the characteristics of the various types in abstract terms, he simply lets us see a genuine representative of each type. Physical characteristics are described, and shortcomings depicted. The method of treatment is given in the same detailed way; and many of these cases have been followed by Dean Holmes far enough so that he has been able to observe the results of the remedies that have been applied. This is the mode of procedure throughout the book, which gives it a very objective, concrete and practical value.

The parent, teacher, medical inspector, or clinician can use Dean Holmes' book in much the same way that a botanist, say, would use a key to the flowers he is identifying and classifying. Most books dealing with human nature do not describe types so that they can be recognized by the non-expert. But this is one of the virtues, and it is an important one, of *Backward Children*. It has the further virtue of being written in a sympathetic spirit. The author feels tenderly for these children who in one way or another can not adapt themselves to the situations in which they are placed. No one will doubt that he is eager to instruct those who have to deal with such children how to discover the cause of their abnormality, whether of intellect or of character, and then how to apply effective remedies.

The book is written in a simple graceful style without affectation or pretense. It is particularly free from technical or professional terminology so that the layman can read it with ease and with pleasure.

M. V. O'SHEA.

Madison, Wisconsin.

AUTHOR'S PREFACE

This volume is an inductive study of backward children. It presents in a series of concrete illustrations studies of cases to exemplify the principles and methods underlying the diagnosis, treatment and training of backward children. It aims to describe the cases as simply, non-technically and humanly as the subject-matter will permit, in order to be of service to the care-taker of children who does not have a technical education in abnormal psychology. The style is purposely as popular in vein as possible without offending scientific principles or sacrificing scientific exactness in essentials.

The larger consideration is given to those backward children who can be reclaimed. The feeble-minded are touched upon only incidentally and for the purpose of showing the dangers to society lurking in their neglect and misunderstanding by the public. Their separation from the temporarily backward requires a clinical diagnosis of each child. How far such a diagnosis can be carried by the ordinary layman is illustrated and explained.

For aid and advice in writing this volume I am indebted to many friends, to whom, on account of the form of the book, acknowledgment can not always be made in the proper place. Miss Elizabeth E. Farrell, Doctor William Burdick and Doctor L. W. Rapeer most kindly read portions of the manuscript and made valuable suggestions; Mr. Charles K. Taylor permitted me to use some of his material on coffee-drinking and on manual training; Miss Effie Reimensnyder read the whole manuscript. To the Psychological Clinic at the University of Pennsylvania, of which Doctor Lightner Witmer is founder and director, and with whom I was associated a number of years, I owe a large number of the illustrative cases used. To the editor, Doctor O'Shea, I am indebted most of all, for his patience and uniform courtesy, for his suggestions and practical direction, and for his unfailing inspiration.

My hope is that the volume may be of help to those who are striving to help the slow boys and girls in the home or the school, and that it may contribute its mite toward a better understanding of these unwilling laggards and a more sympathetic support of their efforts to march with the great army of their more fortunate fellows.

ARTHUR HOLMES.

State College, Pa.

CONTENTS

CONTENTS—*Continued*

The vital kind of teacher illustrated—Two types
of teachers—A teacher's physical attributes—Her
temperament—Her special training—Her age and
experience—Need of teachers—Rooms—Their location—Equipment in detail—Hints for courses.

BACKWARD CHILDREN

BACKWARD CHILDREN

CHAPTER I

MEASURING RODS FOR CHILDREN

"THERE is a boy," said a school-teacher recently, pointing to a pale-faced, high-browed, well-dressed pupil, "who ought to be at the head of his class, and here he is just above the average!" At such an unpolitic speech made to a visitor in his presence, the boy dropped his head and a deep flush of shame went over his pallid features. The visitor became interested and inquired into the matter. He found that the boy was the only child of the leading physician in the town, a man who had done well materially in his profession, but much better in his matrimonial venture. He had married the richest young woman in the neighborhood, a girl noted for her beauty and for her ambition. She persuaded her husband to try his fortune in a large city, which he did for a few years, but, seemingly, he did not succeed there, and upon the death of his father-in-law, the family returned to the wife's native town.

The Individual Standards.—After Harold's birth, his mother's ambition, disappointed in its so-

1

cial aims, turned to her son, and his education was begun almost from the cradle. He went through the kindergarten, with its training supplemented at home by all the forcing processes his mother could command. When the family returned to their native village, Harold was entered in the public school with his mother's certain conviction that, having had such exceptional opportunities at home and such perfect preparation in kindergarten, he would easily excel his less fortunate fellow pupils.

But his mother was doomed to a second life-disappointment. The boy developed into only an ordinary student. He kept up in his classes, did average work in all his studies, but was not brilliant in any. Though his mother ceaselessly urged him on and held frequent conferences with his teachers, though she superintended his lesson preparation at home, and was often present at his recitations in school, still Harold moved on only at the usual pace. Of course the school and the teachers came in for their share of blame delivered in a thoroughly polite and half-veiled way, but delivered nevertheless. The argument was this: Considering his exceptional opportunities and the intellectual superiority of at least one of his parents, Harold ought to be much farther advanced than he is. In short, Harold was compared with himself or with what he might have been, and he was found wanting. Therefore, he was called "backward," was nagged by his mother and twitted by his teachers, and saved only from open rebellion or complete depression by that same blessed mediocrity which called down all the condemnation upon his head. Possibly, also, his kindly father helped by his comforting way of hinting to his son that, though he was not so brilliant as he was expected to be, yet he was not so bad as he might have been.

Harold was judged by the individual standard. That means that any one who is not developed to his fullest capacity is retarded. His fullest capacity is what he might have been according to the judgment of himself or of others who know him. According to that standard all sincere persons must feel themselves retarded; for none of us will affirm that we have had the fullest opportunity possible, nor that we have availed ourselves fully of the opportunity we did have. Hence, by that standard, we are all backward.

The Social Standard in the Home.—Quite different is the story of another boy who lived in a family of two brothers and two sisters in an ordinary home where the children had the usual liberty to follow their own bent. Ernest was the unusual child. He was the dreamer of the family, so called because of his vacant and aimless way of doing things at home. At an age when his brothers and sisters could get up in the morning, wash their faces, comb their hair, and dress themselves without aid from any one, helpless Ernest would have to be pulled out of bed by his energetic mother, washed

and partly dressed by her, and almost driven down
to breakfast. When he went to school, he was
usually late and always the last. The distraction of
that mother can well be imagined. She had to pre-
pare breakfast for her husband who had to go to
work, and get ready five children with all their odds
and ends, one of whom was so exasperatingly slow
that a saint would be driven to desperation by him.
In other home affairs, Ernest was the same. He
either would not or could not learn to do the chores
required of him; he could hardly ever run an errand
and come back on time; he would forget half the
articles he should bring from the store; he dawdled
over everything; he never touched a tool or performed a piece of manual work heartily and energetically. He was never so happy as when he could
curl up in a big chair or sprawl on the floor over a
book.

At school his reputation was different. While
still slow-moving and phlegmatic, his mind worked
with remarkable precision; his ideas were translu-
cent; his memory retentive; knowledge came easily
to him; lessons were treated seriously, and though
Ernest took his own time about beginning them,
once he was started, his attention was absorbing and
he never stopped studying until the printed word
was a part of the fiber of his being. As a result, he
was easily the best pupil of his class, the delight of
his teachers, the pride of the school. At home, his
practical father and mother shook their heads in

grave doubt; at school his teachers predicted for him a rosy future.

Was Ernest really backward or not? What is the reason for such a clash of judgments? Simply this: he was the victim of a double standard of judgment in retardation. At home he was behind his brothers and sisters in self-help and chores. He learned how to do them slowly and he continued to do them slowly and slovenly after he learned them. At school he was deliberate in his study but he was gifted with one of those rare minds that proceeds without a halt in the acquisition of knowledge and retains without a flaw what it learns. Therefore, in the long run he learned many times more than the other pupils. As a result, at home, he was "retarded"; at school, "advanced."

More Accurate Standards.—Because family judgments are lacking in exactness, men have tried to formulate others. Because a child goes to school and because in school backwardness becomes such a vital matter, the problem of pedagogical retardation has received much attention. Two general standards or criteria for judging pedagogical retardation have been used. The first, called the age-and-grade method, calls all children normal who are six years old and in the first grade, or seven years old and in the second grade, and so on; but in actual practise it allows one year more than the usually allotted time for a grade before calling a child retarded. Generalized, the matter might be stated thus: Every child that begins school at the legal age and is promoted regularly with its class is normal; every child who is two years or more behind the grade it should be in for its age is backward. The two-years' allowance instead of one is made because the legal age for entering school varies with locality; because again some children start to school six months or more after their legal age for entrance; and because, still further, it has been found that a smaller allowance would place an overwhelmingly large number of school children in the backward list. Even allowing the two-year rule, about one-third of the school children in the United States are retarded.

The Second Criterion is the Progress of the Scholar.—According to this standard a normal pupil is one who takes one year, or the regularly scheduled time, and no more, to complete a grade, no matter how old he is when he starts to school. At first sight this seems to be a much juster criterion. For it would appear, and it has been continually argued, that the older child who begins school-life later than he ought legally to do will make more rapid progress in his work and ultimately either catch up with or else pass by the younger pupil. The two sides of the question have been treated by Doctor Leonard Ayres, who comes to the conclusion that the two methods really do not disagree very materially in their results. One is as fair to the facts as the other. "Neither the age standard nor the progress standard of measuring retardation," says

Doctor Ayres, "exaggerates the extent of the evil. On the average, results for a considerable number of cities are equal by both methods." The whole problem which at first sight seems reducible to such simple terms, turns out to be exceedingly complex. It will take years of patient labor to arrive at certain and well-accepted results.

The Standards of the Playground.—In the case of Ernest just described, it will be noted that both his parents and his teachers tacitly assumed that the real criterion of backwardness lay beyond his school and his home in the great world in which he would work out his ultimate success in life. His parents, knowing only one avenue to success and that manual labor, were very dubious about their dreaming son's future. His teachers, victims of the limitations of their profession, assumed that there was also only one road to success and that lay through book-learning.

Much more significant for the future, it seems to me, is the estimate made of a child by his fellows on the playground. There are many reasons for this, but I will point out only two. First, regarding the child himself, he is acting spontaneously; he is urged on by the forces resident within himself; he is trying, all unconscious of theories about education, or any future ambitions, or any artificial rewards or punishments, to express all that is in him. Further, it is his own world in which he is making his place. Therefore, it fits him better than any other that he is compelled to live in. Taking these two phases of play together, we see the child as he is. We can therefore make a better and surer estimate of him than when he only partially exhibits his real nature. We know that in play he is not holding back reserves of energies; that he is not failing because he lacks interest, because he is indifferent through wilfulness or a desire to do something else. In play he expresses his last atom of energy; he will run his race, or chase his ball, until he falls in his tracks. All of us have heard of girls who dropped dead jumping the rope. None of us has ever heard of a girl who dropped dead washing dishes. No girl can. She will faint first and so save her life. Play alone can exhaust all her energies. Therefore, we can judge the child more truly on the playground than anywhere else, both for the present and the future. Still, the judgment is our judgment.

Another reason why the play standard is valuable is this: from it we get the judgment of the child's peers. Their judgment is not explicit; perhaps they may never have had the slightest conscious acquaintance with retardation in their lives, nor even know how to pronounce the word; they may not know that a comrade is backward, but they feel it, and act it. As they react upon one another in their jostling play-world each atom of humanity inevitably settles into its proper place with the fatality of potatoes on the way to market. As the forces of nature fit the stars to their undeviating orbits and the glaciers to their rocky beds, so do these youngsters fit each companion to his groove. Such classifications of children are as accurate as they are unconscious and as significant as they are unprejudiced. Fathers and mothers may be blinded by their love, teachers by the mechanics of their profession, and neighbors by their ambitions for their own offspring, but the clear-eyed citizens of boy-ville and girl-ville look on one another without pride or prejudice and judge one another without fear or favor in the largest and most general aspects of their lives.

Not too much weight can, therefore, be given to the place secured by a child in his own world of unsupervised play. The difficulty of applying such judgments to our problem lies in the fact that they so far have not been formulated. They are not only vague but unexpressed in language or symbol. As yet, no genius among adults has arisen to make them exact, to transform them into systems and invent apparatus for making the standards of the playground applicable to mental diagnosis.

Science Will Refine Upon Popular Standards. —Science may come and observe these popular judgments; she may some day take them and refine them and erect them into systems, but it is doubtful if she can ever really improve upon them. The reason for her helplessness is to be found in the vagueness and incomprehensiveness of the "general intelligence" to be measured. What is intelligence? Is it a single faculty? Surely not; for idiots often possess marvelous musical and mathematical faculties. Is it reason? Philosophers reason to perfection, yet are the most impracticable people; so impracticable that they may starve where another man will live well. For witness, read DeQuincey's account of his starving period in London, when he walked the streets for days, being kept alive only by the earnings of his Anne, and never once did it occur to him even to ask for work! Is intelligence one faculty or many faculties? Is it not more a proper balance among many faculties? If it is, and that seems to be the truest answer, then immediately it can be seen how difficult it will always be to measure this balance under artificial conditions. Added to this is the fact that any mental examination must also labor under the circumstance that even in the smallest bit of human knowledge *all* the mental processes are involved; that it is impossible to isolate reasoning, or imagination, or volition, and to consider each one separately and apart from other processes, as in an ideal laboratory experiment. The child is a unit; his consciousness is a unit. Certain phases of the mental process may be emphasized at times, but the others are there and, what is of supreme importance to the teacher or parent, these, for the moment unobserved and unimportant processes, may be the very ones that will make the child eventually a famous and successful man. For example, success in life most frequently depends on coolness and readiness in times of great crises. Artificial tests in clinics and schoolrooms can not, by their nature, afford such situations, while play produces over and over again as a part of its very essence critical moments full of originality and burning with excitement.

The Binet-Simon Standard.—Besides the foregoing standards many others have been worked out for the more accurate measurement of the typical child's mind. One of the most noted in America is the system of the Frenchman Binet, made famous here chiefly by the extensive investigations carried on by Doctor Goddard of the training school at Vineland, New Jersey. These tests attempt to describe in about five simple ways the normal child of any age up to fifteen years. The descriptions are proposed in the form of questions or tasks and in the results thus obtained. The so-called normal child will answer the questions and perform the tasks, or certain proportions of them, in certain ways. The backward child will not perform the tasks or answer the questions suitable to his age, but only those suitable to a younger age. These standards have the qualities of simplicity and of giving their measurements in the ages of normal children.

The danger, illustrated by all the examples in this chapter, of judging persons to be backward when tested by only one standard, appears strikingly in the following single test by the Binet method. A class of school-teachers at a summer school were tried by the twelve-year-old tests in the older Binet series. Not one of twenty-five adult, well-trained, experienced teachers, whose mentality was unimpeachable, could pass all the tests and some of them failed ignominiously in a majority of them. This statement of an experiment is not intended as a criticism of the Binet tests themselves, but as an illustration again of the vital truth not too often to be reiterated that backwardness itself and the significance of backwardness depends upon the standard used to measure it.

The Standards Should Be Clearly Stated and Studied.—So it appears that the standards for measuring backwardness are many. This condition arises from the nature of the case. Unlike measurements of spatial or material objects we are dealing with more or less non-spatial and extremely complex dimensions. We can not take our child to some place where a norm is kept and compare him with that ideal. If we had to measure a stick we could lay down a yard-measure upon it, and see if they agreed. If our measuring stick was in doubt, we could take it to Washington and have it tested to the millionth of an inch and be sure that it was accurate. Unfortunately, in dealing with living children, many difficulties are in the way of such a simple process. First, much of our measuring is subjective and not objective; secondly, the child is such a complex institution, so fearfully and wonderfully made that to classify one child requires literally innumerable measurements; thirdly, and especially, no real, live, *normal* child exists in all the world to whom we can compare our backward child. If only somewhere, in some sort of an institution, a whole row of perfectly normal children, complete for their age in all their physical, mental, moral and social qualities, were kept on exhibition, and we could take any suspected child there and compare him with the model of the same age, then our problem would be marvelously simplified. But such norms do not exist—"Thank goodness," we may almost say under our breath. For if they did all mental progress would be at an end. Beyond them our children could not hope to go. Woe, yea, even worse woe than now, unto any child who would dare to be original! No, no standard of childish perfection exists; and though on that account our problem of measuring backwardness is made illimitably harder, on the whole we agree with the child-world and are glad it is so.

The Meaning of Backwardness.—From the foregoing discussion two important questions may arise. First, what is backwardness? It is altogether a relative matter and not an absolute condition. It is not a mental defect, nor a physical defect, nor a judgment of Providence, nor a quality of the individual inherited or acquired. It is merely a relation. The backward child is behind somebody or lower than he ought to be in some arbitrary scale, according to somebody's judgment. The mere fact that a child is backward is seen immediately as soon as the standard of measurement is stated. Until that is stated backwardness in itself and by itself has practically no significance. That brings up the second question: Is backwardness always to be deplored? Not by any means.

To be behind does not always mean something undesirable. Sometimes it keeps children out of danger, as it did the poor little cripple who hobbled along behind the other children following the Pied Piper, and so got to the mountain too late to be swallowed up forever. That backward child might be taken as an example for backwardness in many other respects. "Your boy is backward," begins the school-visitor, and mother's face falls and her forehead wrinkles, "in smoking," or "swearing," adds the visitor, and mother's face brightens. All depends on *what* a child is backward *in;* and not on the mere fact that he is backward. To express it otherwise, all depends on the standard of backwardness. Before the standard is known the word "backward" means just one thing: the backward one is lagging behind something. As soon as the standard is known, then the implication is clear, and the backwardness is seen to be desirable or undesirable. I have actually seen a young girl of fascinating appearance and an excellent mind brought to a psychological clinic because, according to the strait and strict standards of conduct in her community and the people who had her under their control, she displayed tendencies to degeneracy. The truth was that the girl was simply forward in company, and forward too, only according to the exceedingly conservative judgment of her community. Certainly it would have been better for her, and for all girls, to be "backward" rather than "forward" in society.

In one of the old school-readers there used to be a story about a famine, a bread-line, a crowd of elbowing children, and one little girl, "with patched clothes neat and clean," who always waited with a heavenly meekness till all the other children had seized the largest loaves from the unscientifically managed charity and had departed, leaving Margaret to take the last and smallest loaf. She was a backward child, but her backwardness was not the kind to be condemned. Indeed, such a fine quality was it that one day the rich baker slipped a gold-piece into the smallest loaf and when backward Margaret, as usual, took what was rejected, she found a fortune, and received from her benefactor both the full right to the coin and a homily upon the virtue of backwardness. With this old-fashioned tale we will leave the standards of backwardness and the many measuring-rods applied to this class of children, hoping that the truth of the lesson will come out with fresh force, that all our modern agitation on retardation will not obscure, namely, that backwardness is not wholly or always bad and that it needs to be studied in each individual case to determine its exact nature. To put our inductive study into a form easily assimilable we append the following summary of standards:

I. INDIVIDUAL STANDARDS.—A backward child is one who is not so far advanced as he ought to be, when his birth and opportunities are considered.
II. SOCIAL STANDARDS.
  A. Popular Standards.
    1. In the Home.—A backward child in the home is one who learns at a later age than that of his brothers and sisters how to walk, talk, eat, dress himself, etc. His parents' judgment is the measure.
    2. In the Neighborhood.—A backward child is one who, in the judgment of the neighbors, is behind the other children in their activities. Neighbors usually judge less mercifully than parents and the backwardness is more pronounced if it is noticed by the neighbors.
    3. On the Playground.—A backward child is one who can not play the games children of his age can play, and who therefore plays with younger children.
  B. Scientific Standards.
    1. Among Nations.—A child is backward only when he falls behind the average for his own race or nation. This is the anthropological standard.
    2. In School.
      a. The Age Standard.—A backward child is one who, from any cause whatsoever, is two years or more behind the grade he ought to be in for his age. The pedagogical standard is a child who begins school at the legal age and is promoted regularly with his class. Pedagogical

retardation is a fact, and has nothing to do with causes, is not always a detriment, and should not be condemned until the causes are known.

b. The Progress Standard.—According to this standard a backward child is one who takes longer than the regularly scheduled time to complete one grade, no matter how old he is. In the long run, with many pupils, these two standards give about the same results.

3. In General Intelligence.—According to several systems like the Simon-Binet, De Sanctis, and others, a backward child is one who can not answer certain sets of prescribed questions and do certain tasks presumably fitted to his years. The standard child is one who can do these tasks and give these answers.*

---

* Much of the material in Chaps. 1 and 8 has appeared in the author's *The Conservation of the Child*, J. B. Lippincott Co., Phila., which treats the diagnosis of backward children fully.

CHAPTER II

VARIETIES OF BACKWARD CHILDREN

SOME years ago two new pupils arrived on the same day in the special class of a public school. Whence they came, by what pedagogic highways and byways they had reached their destination and what educational vicissitudes they had suffered on the journey, are only of secondary importance to our purpose of tracing their succeeding history. It is sufficient to say that their schooling began at the usual age, in the usual public schools, and had lasted six years, leaving them both at the age of twelve in the fourth grade. To all appearances, they sprang from about the same social conditions. Their dress and manners marked them as coming from ordinary homes of working people. Their names we will call John and Mary because those are not their names. Carelessly viewed, they were just two quite ordinary, retarded children, superficially alike, noted only for the fact that they helped to swell the thirty-three and seven-tenths per cent. of backward children in American schools.

Their Personal Appearance.—To the hasty observer all difference in personal appearance favored

Mary. She was cleaner and neater, her face and
hands were washed, and her hair carefully parted,
smoothed and tied back with a red ribbon in a large
bow, the loops of which stood out on each side of
her head like butterfly wings. She was pretty, quiet,
ladylike in her manners, and very well behaved. She
came to the special teacher with a good report for
conduct and much praise for her serious efforts to
learn. As she sat there on the seat that first day,
Miss M., the special teacher, found her heart going
out to her in a quiet pity, and she made up her mind
then and there that she would save this fine girl from
any further stigma of failure, if it was at all possible.

John was not nearly so fortunate. His personal
appearance was altogether against him. Boy-like,
his face and hands were not very clean, his hair was
unkempt, his clothes were untidily worn. His manner and manners were both bad. His face wore a
sullen and sometimes defiant look, and when he
moved, it was with a listless, unwilling, slouchy gait.
When he spoke his voice was peculiarly flat and
dead, but frequently rising quickly and easily into
a querulous, irritated tone. The shape of his nose
and his open mouth were sure signs of adenoids,
past or present, which his teacher later found, had
been just recently removed, so recently that the other
signs—crooked teeth, dulled hearing, stoop shoulders, flat chest and general debility, with the lus-
terless eye and vacuous face—were still very much

in evidence. He came with no such good report for
conduct as Mary had brought. By his former teachers he was counted careless, irritable, inattentive,
and had been getting worse instead of better in the
last years of his schooling, despite the hope of improvement through the adenoid operation. The
hope was slow to materialize and John was sent to
the special class.

The Results.—Space and time will not permit
me to give every detail of these two children's pedagogical treatment and training in the next two years.
It must suffice to say that they received the teaching
in a modern special class. The manual work was
first tried. Here in the beginning Mary distinctly
excelled John. She seemed to have a positive genius
for basket weaving. The first one she ever produced
in her life—a small, bowl-like structure—was as
neatly woven, as symmetrically turned and shaped
as any teacher's heart could desire, and loud were
the praises, both in school and at home, that the
amiable and lovable Mary received for her evident
skill and application.

Poor John started bravely, but his interest slack-
ened, his fingers got in his way, he made mistakes,
became excited, then irritated, had to do it over
again, and finally finished a pitiable specimen, out
of shape, begrimed with sweat and tears, and not
fit for exhibition anywhere. It was a sorry sight
though the extremities of its faults were mercifully
covered by the patient charity of his teacher and her

assurance, into which her heart could not enter very warmly, that he would do better next time.

In many other exercises it was not different. Wherever rhythm in any form was involved, Mary fell into it naturally and smoothly. In singing she was not only quick to catch the tune, and to follow it in her sweet, clear voice, but she readily committed the words to memory. She could recite poetry, too, and loved the weekly memory-gems required in school. Her reading was excellent, in fact, good enough to permit her to read easily in a higher grade. Her writing, too, was good in the sense that the letters were well formed and fair to the eye. On the whole, as Miss M. said, if it had not been for her hopelessness in arithmetic and a certain lack of vigor in attacking original situations and in dealing with abstract problems of all kinds, Mary was one of the most satisfactory pupils in the class. At least, Miss M. said that at first. In the course of two years she was surprised to note how little Mary improved in these respects. By dint of much personal attention in school and at home, she did make some progress. Always docile and earnest, she won sympathy and approbation everywhere. As it was evident that she could never learn much arithmetic, it was decided, that since she was a girl, she should be promoted without it. Her other mental work, dependent upon memory, was fair, and her manual work always most excellent. For that she was highly praised, and from that commendation, together with

the adolescent ripening of her mental powers, came
a new-found confidence, which diffused itself
through all her other efforts, and united with her
unfailing willingness, carried her back into the
grades, and at fifteen Mary left school, not graduated, but with the praise of her teachers and with
no suspicion that she was deficient except in one or
two restricted, and, to a girl, not very important
subjects. Yet within two years after Mary left
school and went to work in a box factory, she was
sent by the juvenile court to an institution for the
feeble-minded to be all the rest of her life, a ward of
the state, an apathetic moron, wrecked in life and
morals, a source of sorrow to her parents, and a potential danger to society.

As for John, he stumbled along through the first
months of his special class with varying successes
and failures, in which failures predominated. The
effect of his failures upon the patience of his
teacher was heightened by his irritability, wilfulness,
carelessness, and general bad behavior. Miss M.
struggled on with him only because a few gleams of
ability here and there occasionally flashed out of his
otherwise bunglesome efforts. Basket weaving, he
did not like; singing, he hated with a schoolboy's
lusty hatred of anything cultural and beautiful.
Wood-working was more to his liking and his accomplishments therein really saved his career. As
he worked at carpentry through the months, his
physical condition improved; he took pride in his

work; he was anxious to be at it and he did his lessons in books faithfully so as to get to the bench. Gradually his whole being and activities improved and in two years he went back to the grades, gripped the meaning of things with vigor, developed into a healthy boy, entered a manual training high school at sixteen, and after one year there went out into the world to become a joiner-apprentice in a car shop, where he is to-day, a promising young man.

What was the difference between these two that made such a tragic difference in their lives? Simply and only the difference between permanent and temporary retardation, between feeble-mindedness and pedagogical backwardness due to removable defects; and this difference might have been detected by the skilled teacher and much of its terrible consequences to the girl and to her parents and to society might have been anticipated and prevented. More than that, these are only two of the many cases identical in the one great essential, coming before the teachers of our schools every day. Because teachers do not understand that from one-half of one per cent. to four per cent. of their pupils are feeble-minded, and because they do not have the ability to recognize slight degrees of feeble-mindedness, they not infrequently labor with such unfortunate pupils only to hide their defects temporarily and to expose them eventually to the rigors of the world peculiar to such defective mental and moral natures.

Two Great Varieties of Retardation.—Now

that we have seen something of the meanings attaching to the word "backward," we will turn to a study of the varieties of the phenomenon itself. Complexity and not simplicity confronts us, a complexity in the condition itself to be overcome as far as possible by simplicity in classification. For our purpose a very simple and untechnical classification of backward children might be made, one that will both seize upon the essential difference between two great classes of the retarded ones, and will also at the same time serve the practical end of education. That end is the future of the backward child. We want him to grow up and take his place in the world as a self-supporting and self-respecting citizen. Can he do it? With all his present defects, mental and physical, can he be so treated and so taught that eventually he will become a full-fledged citizen of the republic? That is our practical question and upon it we can base our simple classification of all backward children into those *temporarily* backward and those *permanently* backward. The first will include all those children retarded on account of removable defects; the second will include all that growing army of unfortunate little people whose defects are deeply seated within their very being beyond the present philosophy of man to understand. Hence, it is seen at once how vital it is to all concerned that this distribution be made in the case of every backward child, and be made as early as possible. Upon it depends all its future treatment and training. Without such a distinction teachers and parents may go on trying to teach their charges things impossible to learn and things positively hurtful, and at the same time rob them of the opportunity to learn other things for which their capacities are suited and through which they would reach their highest attainments and most joyful service. On this point too much emphasis can not possibly be· laid. I have seen a child brought apparently to the lowest stages of idiocy by the neglect of her parents who deemed it impossible to teach her because she was permanently retarded. Yet that same child, under medication and with skilful teaching, changed within a few years to a most polite, beautiful little lady, capable of rudimentary reading and writing and seemingly at that time destined to grow into full womanhood. On the other hand, I have seen a child driven by her mother into almost complete mental bankruptcy by attempting to force the poor benumbed mind to read and write and do arithmetic when such mysteries would be ever beyond the ken of this manually capable and housewifely little girl. In both cases the children suffered; one from neglect and the other from overstraining, and both from the same cause, namely, the lack of understanding that differences, absolute and lifelong, exist among backward children.

Further Study of Temporarily Retarded Children.—After we have made this basal and vital distinction between the two kinds of retarded children, we have still further sub-classifications to make. These finer divisions chiefly concern the teacher. They have arisen from the needs of the class-room, and therefore fit in very well with our purpose of classifying backward children by their future ability to support themselves in ordinary society. First, some of these children begin to improve immediately after the removal of their defects. For example, a retarded girl with a good personal history was found to be suffering with enlarged tonsils, poor eyes, and crooked and decayed teeth. Her eyes and tonsils were treated and almost immediately she showed improvement in other ways. Her appetite improved, she became less susceptible to colds, her teeth grew straighter; she was promoted at school and maintained her position in her class without further trouble.

A boy nine years of age, after going to school three years, had reached only the second grade. He was good in some studies. He usually made eighty to ninety per cent. in spelling, but he could not subtract twenty-five from fifty, nor eighteen from twenty-five orally. He could say over words in the second reader, but did not seem to obtain any meaning from the process. His teachers stated that he was not interested in school work and was very careless about everything. Possibly there was some connection between his carelessness and his habit of rising at 5 A. M. to deliver papers, but his chief trouble lay in his defective vision.

Twice in six months his eyes were examined and glasses fitted to them at a clinic. The improvement was immediate and continuous. In the same class with the same teacher, he changed entirely and applied himself so well that he became a good scholar in all his studies, and in geography and history, his former bugbears, he secured grades of eighty-five and ninety-four per cent. respectively. He represents the class of children very numerous in school whose backwardness is due to physical defects and who respond immediately to proper medical treatments.

A similar case is a girl nine years of age, in the third grade, whose retardation was not marked enough to be noted in school but marked enough to attract the notice of her parents. It gave them some uneasiness because the child had suffered congestion of the brain when she was five and again when she was eight, and because they feared that her increasing backwardness was due to some mental derangement.

An examination revealed no signs of mental abnormalities, but it did reveal poor eyesight, enlarged tonsils, adenoids and a consequent sore throat. When the adenoids were removed and her eyes fitted with glasses, the child changed immediately for the better. Her health improved greatly. The signs of nervousness disappeared and with them her disposition changed from melancholy to cheerfulness, from constant irritability to normal good humor,

and her conduct from disobedience and rebellion
to willing and happy effort to please. Her mental
improvement was equally marked. Lessons that
formerly were labored over with weariness, discouragement and tears, now came easily. Her music lessons, formerly an equal trial to her and her mother,
became seasons of special enjoyment. So rapidly
did she advance in music that she soon surpassed her
mother in accomplishment. All of this change was
due to the treatment and not to training. Her case
illustrates what can be done by wise and watchful
parents who look for causes of conduct and intelli-
gently seek remedies at children's clinics before the
advance of diseases causes trouble at school.

Rapidly Recoverable Cases.—Jack, at eleven
years, promised to be a ne'er-do-well. He could not
learn in school. He was discouraged and his relatives were discouraged, too. He did not know what
was the matter and nobody else seemed to know.
He had floundered along for five years in the public
school of his small town and was only in the second
grade. He could not read in a second reader; his
spelling was poor; his grammar was atrocious; his
writing a combination of poor spelling, worse grammar and illegible penmanship.

Yet he was a good boy, obedient, affectionate
and thoughtful of others. He loved pets, and had a
dog, some rabbits and chickens, all of which he
cared for faithfully. He built them pens, and fussed
and worked with them every spare hour he had.

At eleven years of age he was brought to a clinic by his mother. They lived in a country town or he would have been brought before. There it was found he had enlarged tonsils, but his chief trouble was poor eyesight. His tonsils were removed and glasses were fitted to his eyes and he was entered in a special summer class in the city in which his physical activities were given free opportunity. He was very good in gymnastic drills and in swimming. Carpentry also served to rouse his dormant faculties and to stimulate his interest in study. With his eyesight improved he found reading much easier and took to simple history. In six weeks he went back home, and in the fall entered the regular third grade, where his progress fully satisfied everybody. He went through the primary grades, and at sixteen, on account of the absence of his father from home, he took full charge of their small farm and ran it successfully. The proper diagnosis, treatment, and brief special training changed this boy from a tramp in embryo to a wholesome and worthy member of the community, capable in a pinch, of becoming the support of the family.

Jack illustrates a second group among temporarily retarded children. Unlike the first group, they do not show immediate improvement on removal of their physical defects. They start to school, fall behind in their grades, are examined and found to have a number of physical defects, or to be badly situated in a poor neighborhood, or live in a poor home where they do not have enough to eat. When they are treated medically or surgically, or removed from their bad neighborhoods, or their homes, they then require manual training or individualized instruction to arouse again their dormant and temporarily stagnated faculties. Such children improve and eventually return to their regular classes, graduate from school and go out into the world ready to make a living.

The Slowly Recoverable.—Julia was a discouraging pupil. She was thirteen years old with six years of schooling to her credit, during which many and sundry teachers had wrought upon her to see what they might make of her meager mind. Four years she had submitted meekly to regular grade instruction, learning a little at first and then losing that little gradually until she went into a special class. For two years individual instruction, with all the accessories of equipment and manual work, were brought to bear upon her with practically no results. Then she was taken to a clinic for diagnosis, where a number of complications were discovered.

The girl was very small for her age, a pale anemic child, with bad teeth, poor eyesight, enlarged adenoids and tonsils. She was dull and sleepy, subject to spells of stubbornness, heart-breaking to an ambitious teacher, but otherwise of an excellent moral character. Glasses were fitted to her eyes, her teeth were treated, and her nervous and intestinal troubles received the proper medication. Then she went back to the special class.

Now the two chief values of all special classes are found in the large amount of attention given to each pupil in the small classes and in fitting the instruction to the peculiar needs of each pupil. Julia liked to sew, to take physical exercise, to play games and to sing. So she received regular daily training in all these arts. Nothing special or peculiar was introduced into the methods of teaching her these common accomplishments. It was the fact that she was learning the things she could learn that counted. The effect of such exercises began soon to appear. They showed first in her constantly and rapidly improving physical condition. Health came to her body, blood to her cheeks, brightness to her eyes, and energy to her muscles. Along with health came improvement in her disposition. Her stubbornness just evaporated under the sunshine of daily wellbeing.

Finally her power to perform mental work began to grow. Concentration, always dependent upon physical power in some form or other, increased with the increase of health and strength. Julia began to learn, and the joy of developing common to all children when they grow came to her. Four months of strenuous training were required to stem the tide of retrogression and to return her to the regular third grade. That of course was far below her normal grade and it will take several years of

hard work yet to bring her up anywhere near to the
standard. It seems a profound pity that so many
years were wasted before a clinic examination was
made, but we must remember that it was the clinic
that started her right and assured her teachers of
ultimate victory.

Julia, unlike some of the boys and girls just described, belongs to a class of slowly recoverable
temporarily retarded children. They are by all odds
the most difficult cases to diagnose and to train. In
their general appearance and mental powers they
seem to belong not to the temporarily retarded but
to the permanently retarded, for whom little can be
done. They often suffer from a multitude of defects—poor vision, bad hearing, enlarged tonsils,
adenoids, decayed teeth and malnutrition; they tire
easily, are irritable or apathetic, without ability to
pay attention, idlers, slovenly, falling into mischief,
centers of disturbance and constant drains upon the
teacher's time and patience. All of their physical
defects may be remedied, they may be placed in the
best of special classes and yet for a long time their
mental awakening is beyond the hope of all but the
most faithful and experienced. Gradually they take
hold; some detail of manual labor appeals to them
and they do it with a new pleasure. From that,
step by step, the experienced teacher leads them out
into wider and more intricate pieces of manual work
until at last the day comes when the gulf between
the concrete task and the abstract symbol, between

training and teaching, is bridged and the road to the higher learning lies open once more. The progress may still be slow, but the upward march is sure, and the outcome, though possibly long delayed, is certain. No single group of children requires so much patience, so much skill in diagnosis and training, and so much abounding faith in the infallibility of psychological analyses as does this group. If to their mental backwardness are added moral delinquencies, then indeed is their lot a hard one. For it is so easy for the uninformed parent or unprepared teacher to explain the whole trouble by saying, "He is just bad; that's what is the matter with him," but utterly forgetting that in this case the badness is not at all a *cause*, but merely a symptom, or a concomitant, of the backwardness.

These children are often confused with the feebleminded, and hence in some cases great cures of the feeble-minded are heralded by instructors who are not skilful in making diagnoses. This is not to be wondered at since the physical appearances and mental attributes of these children very closely approximate those of the truly feeble-minded. The resemblances are only superficial, while the differences are profound. It is in this realm that so much waste of energy and so much confusion in theory is to be found. Teachers will insist that middle-grade imbeciles, for example, can be taught to read and write, because they have received children diagnosed as middle-grade imbeciles into their classes and have succeeded in teaching them to read and write. It is perfectly evident to those who understand that if, by definition, a middle-grade imbecile is one who can not be taught to read and write, then children called middle-grade imbeciles and who still learn to read and write are not what they are diagnosed to be. That mistakes of this kind should frequently occur is not at all surprising when we consider how few skilled mental diagnosticians there are and how many mental diagnoses are made by laymen and by others with very little special training. It is, therefore, highly necessary that the teacher of special children should keep herself clear from confusion of this sort. She should maintain her poise of mind and retain her clear discrimination between temporarily retarded and the permanently retarded and neither waste her time by spending useless energy on the latter nor exhibit undue exhilaration over the reclamation of the former. Especially must she be on her guard against asserting that a feeble-minded child, who very naturally makes exceedingly rapid progress after surgical and medical treatment, with a little intensive training, is not feeble-minded, but only temporarily backward. Just recently in an institution I came across a girl manifestly feeble-minded, who six or seven years ago under the care of an expert, received the proper medical and surgical treatment, and then was placed with a special teacher. Under this tutelage the girl progressed very rapidly. She seemed to awaken to new life intellectually and emotionally. Her physical condition, her disposition, her character and her conduct all leaped forward in unison. She soon entered a grade in a regular public school where, though she was much retarded pedagogically, she kept pace with her class and made good progress. Gradually, however, her first rapid strides grew slower and shorter until finally she reached her upper limit of intellectual growth and has remained there stationary ever since. Several observers were deceived by her first remarkable advancement and prematurely concluded that she was entirely normal.

CHAPTER III

A SPECIAL-CLASS teacher of long experience was one day confronted with the worst case she had ever seen. He was a boy of eleven years whose parents had recently moved into the neighborhood and had entered their son in the regular grade, where the teacher had tried her best with him, and had finally appealed to the principal to relieve her of this hopeless case by placing him in the special class for backward children. So the principal brought him to the special teacher and gave her as much as he knew of the boy's family, personal and pedagogical history.

The parents were ordinary hard-working people of good stock; his brothers and sisters were all normal and several were in school doing well. The boy himself had never suffered with any specially severe disease like diphtheria, nor any that left bad mental consequences behind, nor did he suffer from epileptic fits, St. Vitus' dance, nor nervousness, though he had a few more than his share of children's ordinary diseases like measles, mumps, chicken-pox and the like, and continually suffered from colds, sore throat, toothache and occasionally earache.

His school-life presented nothing very marked in particular, though on the whole it was bad. He started to school at six; at first made good progress, but contracted the measles and was out of school for six weeks, and after that seemed to lose interest and to fall behind until he was only in the third grade, and was that far along more by grace than by merit. He seemed to be generally and hopelessly retarded. He was poor in everything. Apparently he did not try; he was dull, stupid, inattentive, forgetful, irritable, stubborn, irregular in his attendance, annoying when he was in school, and latterly suspected of truancy when he was out. In it all, he did not seem to be particularly mentally defective; some of his teachers asserted he was feeble-minded, while others said he could learn if he would. Such was his history when he came to the special teacher.

Diagnosis of the Case.—As I said, this teacher had both training for and experience in her work. Though this boy seemed a hopeless case, she proceeded in her usual systematic and efficient manner. She wasted no time calling him names nor labeling him. She did not stop to ask if he was "really retarded." That he *was* pedagogically retarded was a patent fact. *Her* business was ultimately to restore him to the grades if that was possible. Her immediate task was to decide if that was possible. To decide that she must find the *causes* of this boy's backwardness. Her experience assured her the causes were either in the boy himself or in his environment.

Environmental Causes.—In his environment there was nothing unusually bad. His home was not rich, but it was a good one. His brothers and sisters were normal. His schooling had been the usual one, and his brothers and sisters had succeeded with the same schools, lessons and teachers he himself had had. The neighborhood in which he lived and played was typical, neither very good nor very bad. His companions were not noted for their delinquencies, though he had in the last year fallen in with a crowd of boys who formed the worst element of the school and who numbered among them some of the truants and incorrigibles. But, on the whole, it seemed clear that the cause of this boy's decline in school work was not due to environment, but to something in him. Was that something a mental defect, as a number of his teachers said, or a physical defect?

The Physical Examination.—For answer the teacher turned to the boy himself. He had come slouching in behind the principal and had stood fingering his cap and casting furtive glances around the room and over the other fifteen children of various ages in the ungraded class, while the principal gave the teacher a rapid account of her new charge's life and present condition. When the principal left, in answer to the teacher's word, Joe—we will call

him, though that is not his name—shuffled up to
the desk and stood before her. No wonder others
thought him hopeless. Almost every line of his personal appearance and posture spoke loudly of physical and mental inefficiency. To the acute eyes of
the teacher his clothing manifested the struggle going on between a mother, neat and energetic, still
hoping to keep up a high standard of appearance,
and the slow but sure inroads of mental retrogression in the boy. His clothes were good, somewhat
worn, carelessly put on and slovenly carried on
a slouching frame. Great perpendicular wrinkles
creased his coat at the shoulders; his soft shirt collar, though clean and white, was pulled out of shape,
with one wing over and the other under his coat
lapel; his four-in-hand necktie had slipped down
from his collar and the ends hung outside his vest;
his stockings were not pulled up smoothly; his shoe-
strings were only partly laced. The struggle between a mother's will and a backward boy's listless
indifference was patent everywhere in his clothes.

The whole effect was accentuated and heightened
by his posture. He stood with his arms hanging at
his sides, stoop-shouldered, flat-chested, his shoulder-blades outstanding, betraying in every attitude
he took the lassitude and weakness due to lack of
oxygen, to faults of digestion and assimilation, and
to the poisons of fatigue. The teacher's trained eye
went over him from head to foot, noting in detail
every characteristic, eliminating the unimportant

and non-essential, marking down in her retentive memory the vital essentials, and letting these tell their story to her unbiased and disciplined judgment.

Her survey began with his hair, naturally thick and glossy, but now dead and unruly, showing evidences of having been wetted and combed that morning, but later mussed by a careless adjustment of the cap, which the embarrassed boy now swung backward and forward in nervous little semicircles. The shape of his head, the size and shape of his ears, eyes, nose, mouth and jaws were all *naturally* normal, as the teacher could discern by her analysis, though some features were marred by defects. The sallow complexion, the drooping eyelids, the vacuous expression of face, and the listlessness of every movement betokened either imbecility or the total result of many advanced physical defects.

Signs of Adenoids.—To decide whether Joe was permanently or only temporarily retarded, Miss F., the teacher, knew that his physical defects must first be diagnosed and removed and a chance be given for his native powers to appear and to be developed by proper training in a special class. To begin the analysis of Joe's real condition by her own observation, Miss F. made a few gentle and kindly inquiries, placed him in a seat well up in front, and gave him some simple busy-work which would take his mind off of himself and yet not make so great a demand upon his attention that his activity would

obscure his real self-expression. In the meantime
Miss F. continued her careful and systematic examination, while Joe, blissfully ignorant of it, proceeded to adjust himself to his new surroundings.
Very quickly the teacher noted the most potent
adenoid signs. Experience taught her what trains
of evil effects to expect in addition to these patent
defects.

Because adenoids are so common, because they
are so intimately connected with retardation, because their mental effects so closely resemble feeble-
mindedness, and because their accompanying physical defects are so numerous, we will describe briefly
what Miss F. saw in them. So true is the last statement that we can almost say that a study of adenoids and their symptoms will cover nearly all
the non-contagious, most common physical defects a
child-trainer will ordinarily be called on to discover.

Adenoids are really tonsils always normally present and giving trouble only when they swell by over-
growth and hang down from the rear wall of the
passage between the throat and the nose, forming
lobes of pulpy, red, spongy masses like several rai-
sins on a stem, the whole about as large as the end
of an adult's finger. In that position they obstruct
breathing, compelling the sufferer to bring in his
supply of oxygen directly through the mouth instead
of by the radiator-like, dust-gathering passages of
the nostrils, where the air is warmed and cleansed.
The first external signs of adenoids to be looked for

by the teacher, though of course others may precede
this one, is the thickening of the *bridge* of the nose
without depression. The bony bridge simply widens
by swelling at each side and gradually joins the
cheek like a hill melting into a plain. The nostrils,
because of their disuse in breathing, do not develop,
remain narrow and small, lose their fine chiselings,
and take on an infantile, putty-like, unfinished appearance. If the whole nose is inspected sharply, it
appears as if the bridge and the nostrils did not
match, as if the bridge was several years older than
the nostrils.

Very quickly following this thickening of the
nose bridge comes the mouth breathing. It may be
harder to detect than one thinks. Children are
scolded so frequently for holding their mouths open
that some of them acquire the habit of snapping
their lips shut whenever they look at any one in
authority or a grown person looks their way. As a
result the mouth appears to be closed most of the
time and the weary-worn, labor-saving device, "It
is just a habit!" stops further parental endeavor and
throws the burden of the matter on the already
overburdened frame of the patient sufferer, a patient and a sufferer in more senses than one. The
sympathetic observer will secretly watch the child
when he—she, I was just going to say, because girls
more than boys suffer from all forms of suppression—when he is off guard. The best time is during the child's sleep. Parents, however, are so loath

to admit that anything is wrong with their own children and usually feel so much of a repugnance, not to say fear, of an operation that unfortunately their witness fails where it is needed most. However, the matter can not be long in doubt with anything like observation, and at any time the diagnosis of a modern throat specialist will settle the matter. He will use a small mirror and a light to look up into the arch of the post-nasal cavity or explore it with his finger. The first method the lay person is almost always unable to use, and the second, for reasons many and obvious, he is wholesomely advised not to try.

The open mouth of the adenoid case is not due at first to a dropping of the lower jaw, but a shortening of the upper lip. The fashion plates of school misses, or the stereotyped faces of feminine beauties found everywhere to illustrate the traditional fragile and clinging type of woman, offer the best opportunties to study the ideal adenoid upper lip. For some reason, possibly because of the "weaker sex" theory, the world has forced to some extent the adenoid face and almost wholly the adenoid upper lip upon the womanly woman, and the firm normal upper lip upon her anti-type, the "strong" woman. All such perversions of nature showered upon us in daily arts of advertisements and illustrations tend to confuse our minds and obscure the defects from which children suffer. Though the upper lip is first affected, it is not long before the lower lip also suffers. It thickens, tends to roll out and down, falling with the lower jaw. The lip thus exposed to the air, and deteriorating with the rest of the body, becomes chapped and cracks, often being covered with seams which open and bleed easily. Usually it takes a long time after the adenoids are removed for the lips to recover their normal shape and beauty.

Adenoids, enlarged tonsils and crooked teeth follow one another almost with the fatality of cause and effect. The connection is certain if the adenoids develop at or before the time of second teething, at about seven years of age. This is due to the peculiar effect adenoids have upon the shape of the jaws. The upper jaw assumes a V-shaped appearance, losing its curve and tending to a point in front. Some writers believe it is a reversion to the animal jaw it so closely resembles, others, that it is chiefly due to the pressure of enlarged tonsils. Naturally such a malformation crowds the teeth together and out of line. The upper front incisors jamb together and overlap; then the canines, or eye teeth, come in either inside or outside of their proper places and form "tushes"; the other teeth adjust themselves to their crowded quarters as best they can, and often the jawbones are bent up or down so that either the front teeth or the back will not come together at all.

Under such conditions chewing is agony at worst and ill-paying labor at best. Bolting the food gives immediate relief and future digestive retribution, neither of which, with all the parental admonitions and threats thrown in, will be efficacious until the child's teeth are restored by a dentist to their proper grinding positions. Unless some positive treatment for straightening the teeth is given, the crooked teeth and consequent deformed and ugly mouth will accompany the sufferer through life. Crooked teeth are not misfortunes of fate, but curable defects, and ninety-five per cent. of them are due to adenoids.

Still the category of ills justly ascribed to adenoids is not complete. They rob the body of its most necessary nutrition, food and oxygen. How the food is lost by insufficient chewing due to bad teeth has been described above. Robbing of oxygen seems at first sight a false charge. For is it not easier to breathe through the mouth than through the nose? Why then is not more instead of less air taken in that way? First, because the organism seeks to protect itself against the direct blast of incoming cold and dusty air striking directly upon the irritated membrane of the adenoid throat. Secondly, because of the ease of intake and the reduction of the amount of air, the neck muscles and the inter-rib muscles are not exercised; the ribs sag, the chest flattens, the shoulders droop forward, and the shoulder-blades stand out with remarkable prominence. This whole condition is furthered and heightened by the lassitude and weakness of the body due to lack of oxygen, to faults of digestion and assimilation, and to fatigue. The sallow complexion, the paleness about the lips, the dark furrows under the eyes, and the drooping eyelids, with a weary expression of face and listlessness in every movement, except when quick irritation overcomes the constant disinclination to move, complete the picture of a well advanced adenoid case.

Mental Signs of Adenoids.—The mental signs of adenoids are almost as well marked as the physical ones just described. Irritability is the one first noticed. It is almost impossible for the sufferer to get up in the morning, dress, eat breakfast and get started to school without a quarrel and a cry over something. Ignorant parents attribute such outbreaks to mere temper and frequently assist in the destruction of the child's disposition and nervous system by means of the ever-ready rod. There is no mystical connection between adenoids and irritability. Let any one push a wad of cotton about the size of the little finger end back through his nose so it will lodge in the cavity and obstruct his breathing. Of course, it will compel him to breathe through his mouth. His mouth and throat will become parched, his sleep will be uneasy and broken; all the neighboring membranes will become irritated, and in the morning, just as worn-out nature composes itself for some real sleep, he is called to an arbitrary task and expected to arise immediately, obediently, amiably and gladly, greeting all the household with a happy "Good morning!" Such expectations are against nature. The same explana-

tion applies to wandering and flighty attention, the
second marked symptom of adenoids. The constant
irritation grown so habitual to the child as to be
almost unnoticed by him under ordinary circumstances, comes up into clear consciousness as soon
as he tries to apply his mind to monotonous books.
Everybody has noticed the same phenomenon with
any slight irritant. Excitement drowns out a pain.
But who can study with a pair of tight new shoes
burning his feet? If adenoids are allowed to remain, other more general mental effects follow the
gradual decline of physical strength: a general
mental lassitude, inability to apply the mind, dull-
ness and such low mental power that adenoid cases
of advanced standing are often mistaken for imbecility. It is in this very realm that the most striking cases of recovery from retardation are recorded.

Tests By Reading.—Miss F. finally had Joe
read for her. She gave him a book as easy as the
first reader and let him handle it in his own way.
To free him from embarrassment as much as possible she let him sit in his seat. He seized the book
with both hands, tightened up all the muscles of his
body, began in a high-pitched, falsetto key, with a
peculiar deadened tone in it which his teacher recognized at once as the "adenoid voice." When he
came to a word that he did not quite know, Joe
screwed up his face, squinted his right eye and
swung his head around so that his left eye did all
the seeing. His pronunciation exhibited minor yet

significant peculiarities. He constantly omitted the
"g" in words ending in "ing"; he slurred many
other sounds and often omitted entirely a final syl-
lable with perfect equanimity and entire irresponsi-
bility. Not once did the new teacher stop him, nor
advise him nor correct him.

Joe was elated; so was the teacher. She was sure
now that he had adenoids, almost certain that his
tonsils were enlarged, suspected that he was partially deaf, and felt adequately convinced that he
was near-sighted and that his right eye was far more
affected than his left. The position of his book,
the twisting of his head, shutting one eye in difficult
places, the wrinkles above his eyes across his forehead, all these told her of eye strain and argued for
many other nervous stresses all over his body that
may have led to many, many of his unruly fits and
bad actions. His slurring of syllables without any
consciousness of it, together with the adenoids, argued for partial deafness, and these were seconded
by his peculiarly loud voice. None of these signs
alone would have meant much, but altogether their
cumulative evidence was almost irresistible. His
teacher was not surprised a moment later, when,
without even touching the boy, she faced him to a
window, asked him to open his mouth wide and
pronounce "a" short, as in "rat," while she looked
into his open mouth and saw the red masses on each
side of his throat. Now she was certain of the enlarged tonsils, and also as sure of them as if she

could see the enlarged adenoids hanging in the post-
nasal passage in such a way as to obstruct most effectually any breathing through the nasal passage
provided by nature to warm and strain the incoming
air. A few simple additional tests would make her
also morally certain of the eye and ear defects and
give her the assurance that she could refer this poor
boy to the medical inspector without any fear that
her tentative diagnosis would prove an exaggerated
and unsupported suspicion.

To give the eye tests she simply held up letters
printed in different sized types at certain distances
from the boy's eyes, distances that she had marked
off on the floor by making tests upon normal children. She tried first one eye and then the other.
While her tests were not at all final or official they
were accurate enough to convince her that Joe
needed an oculist. The ear tests were equally simple. She stood Joe up against the wall with his
right ear to the wall, his finger in it and his eyes
shut, and then had him repeat words to her that
she whispered to him while she stood at specified
distances from him. These distances she knew by
former tests. Just to confirm her judgment and to
interest this backward boy—who was receiving, by
the way, a great deal of real education from the
tests—she had him stand before her with his back
to her, close his eyes, and then listen for a watch
which she held concealed in one hand, while she
brought both her closed hands from a distance on

each side of his head toward his ears. As soon as he was sure he heard the watch he raised the hand on the side that he heard it. As she suspected, he was almost entirely deaf in one ear and his hearing was much diminished in the other. It was a revelation to Joe and a matter of keen interest to the other children, though, of course, none of them knew all the results or their entire significance. None of them guessed, for instance, what the teacher knew was true, that much of Joe's stubbornness, stupidity, truancy and pseudo-feeble-mindedness was already explained. Though he did look hopeless, though adenoids choked his breathing passages, and tonsils nearly filled his throat, though both had been instrumental in bringing on the earache and partial deafness, and had further warped his jaws out of shape; though his teeth were decaying and tartarous; though he was bereft of his vitality by this undernutrition and by lack of oxygen because of adenoids; though his eyes were poor, and altogether he seemed a sorry object, still there was hope. Great indeed was the faith that could see a future for this boy, his mouth open, his teeth crooked and decaying, his jaws malformed, his nose thickened at the bridge and undeveloped at the nostrils, his eyes heavy, his hearing impaired, colds and sore throats his weekly lot, his body starving for air and food and proper rest in sleep, his attention flighty, his mind sluggish, his temper quick and easily irritated, his disposition stubborn and rebellious, a child unfit in every respect for schooling or for work, for play or companionship, a ready victim to many diseases and susceptible to bronchitis, pneumonia, and tuberculosis, and yet all his troubles physical and mental, with the exception of a few like his visual defects, could be traced directly or indirectly to adenoids. He, indeed, was an extreme case, but how many other backward children are there that suffer little and much from a few or many of the same physical defects.

Joe's Treatment.—Miss F. knew that it was useless to waste time giving Joe mental tests or trying to proceed with his education while all the avenues to his mind were blockaded effectually against any admission of knowledge. She sent him to the medical inspector of the school, who confirmed all her tentative diagnoses, and referred the boy to specialists and clinics for treatment. Of course Joe's parents were amazed at the condition of their boy. They were plain people who had not found adenoids and enlarged tonsils in their spellers and readers when they went to school and were inclined, like most parents who are moved through fear and prejudice, to charge all advice regarding surgical operations to attempts at experimentation upon their most precious son. But tact and coaxing by the medical inspector, the special teacher and the school nurse, finally won the day, and Joe's mother went with him to the hospital for the throat operation. It was a trying time for the poor woman and a positive epoch in Joe's life. He went bravely enough, with a mixture of weariness and fear and stoicism that did not sit badly upon him. When at last he was undressed and stretched upon the wheeled couch and felt the cone for the ether slipped over his mouth and nose, he almost rebelled, but made a great effort—and knew nothing more for some minutes. The doctor opened his mouth, slipped a curved knife back behind the' soft-palate and with one sweep removed the adenoids forever. The tonsils followed next, both with a great show of blood, and Joe came out of the operating room still asleep. He revived in a few more minutes, and felt first of all the new freedom of a clear breathing passage and an unclogged throat. For a week or more his throat was sore, of course, but that he endured with great fortitude because of new-found pride in being looked up to by other boys who had never been fortunate enough to have adenoids and tonsils and to go into a real hospital for terrible operations! Then there was the tenderness of his mother and his brothers and sisters and the new grave solicitude of his father, and above all the real addition to his moral strength which had come from nobly going through the ordeal and making that final, never-to-be-forgotten decision to stand it all when the etherizing began.

The eye examinations were not at all bad. The "drops" made it impossible for him to see things near by, but they did not hurt. His new glasses were strange at first and he had one or two accidents with them in spite of the admonitions of his mother and the family worry over the cost of repairs. The ear trouble and the catarrh of the nose and throat were the most stubborn and demanded the longest and most patient treatments. But Joe and his mother, inspired by the confidence of Miss F., kept up the work and became familiar with clinics and specialists and inured to waiting in anterooms where the afflicted of the world gather daily. The dentists were Joe's worst enemies. At their hands he suffered many and sundry tortures. Somehow there was not the same glory in submitting to the irritation of getting a tooth filled as there was to going out into the dark unknown by ether, and Joe's protestations were inversely proportionate to the decrease in glory. But at last it was over; the hopeless teeth were drawn, the others were filled, and a band, with little screws at the back, was clamped tightly upon his upper teeth to bring them slowly and as painlessly as possible back to their normal shape.

It was March when Joe came to the special class, and it was the latter part of May before his clinic treatments were finished and he was released from almost daily physical pain and permitted to continue his treatments for ear and catarrh at home, with occasional visits to the doctors. In the meantime he had kept up a broken attendance at school, being excused when necessary for his treatments. His

lessons were irregular and his education but per-
functory during that time. Yet it was wonderful
to see how he was already learning. It seemed as
if many items of knowledge that had been so laboriously instilled into his mind and seemingly forever submerged there came back again. He was
changed physically also. There was a new brightness in his eye, a better color to his cheek, a firmer
position and finer carriage to his body, a better appetite and more visible results from his food. His
mouth was still open and he was far from the boy
he should have been, for ills that gather through
years can not be dispelled in weeks. His new-found
strength of muscle and purpose was exercised
chiefly in the manual and physical work of the special class, where he was not only acquiring skill, but
was also developing interest in both manual and
mental tasks by discovering hitherto unknown con-
nections between the things he learned in books and
the things he liked to do with his hands. Almost
before Joe knew it June had come and with it vacation, the great period of relief to him before, but
this year another momentous occasion in this year
of great experiences.

Joe's Constitutional Treatments.—Through
the never-failing kindness of Miss F., Joe's mother
was recommended to a society and Joe was sent to
the country for the summer in care of a fresh air
organization. How he spent that summer it would
take volumes to tell if everything he did and learned

were put down. It was the first time in his life he had ever been so long in the country. The farm where he stayed was a real farm, with a barn, stable, horses, cows, barnyard, fowls of all kinds, and two puppies just at the playful age, with a pond near by for the boys, who like himself were there for the summer, to swim in; with plenty of good nourishing country food to eat, without the constant temptation to devour candies and ice-cream and to drink soda-water. Indeed, the old burning in Joe's throat that, combined with his under-nourished body, brought on that awful and continual craving for freezing mixtures, or cigarette narcotics, was gone, and in its place came a regular, robust appetite that made a slice of bread, golden-crowned with fresh country butter, look like the most delicious treat that ever made a boy's mouth water in expectation. Back of all this happy vacation life was a system, but of course Joe did not know it. He did not dream that his treatment was constitutional and that the five necessities of his daily life—food, air, sleep, water and play—were all carefully regulated, albeit with such masterly care that the regulative devices were all out of sight.

In the fall when Joe came back to school he was wonderfully changed. His schoolmates hardly knew him, and even Miss F., who had hoped marvels for him, was surprised. He was a healthy, round-cheeked, brown-skinned young savage, as happy and enthusiastic as a boy could be who was tasting that most exhilarating of all experiences, the rapid return of a naturally good constitution to health and strength after a long down-hill journey. He was not yet perfect. The marks of his adenoids were still upon him. His teeth, slowly returning to normal position, were white and clean. Toothache and earache both were things of the past. He had not known a cold since spring airs came. His shoulders were somewhat stooped, but his lips were closed, and it was a positive delight to his teacher to look at the strong mouth, with its curve returning, taking the place of that former unsightly gap in his face. His nose, too, was reshaping itself under the exercise of breathing. He still wore his glasses, and behind them his eyes glowed with new interests and new meaning. His body showed the greatest improvement. He had gained in weight and in muscular vigor; his nervousness had almost disappeared and in its place had come a poise that spoke of self-control and energy ready and anxious to take up and complete the tasks of a boy's life. With it all his temper had changed. He was not sullen, but willing; not stubborn, but docile; not stupid, but eager to learn.

The remnants of his defects, especially his decreasing deafness and his eye defects, kept him for a little time in the special class. There he rounded out his deficiencies rapidly, learned quickly to spell and to read and to do arithmetic sufficiently to return to his grade, entering the fourth grade at the

end of the first half-year. His school progress from
that time on was very good. He not only kept up,
but made some advance, and though he finished the
eighth grade one year behind the usual age, he went
out into the world well equipped with a strong body
and a good mind, and since that time has done well
in a printing office, where his father secured him a
position. Without doubt he will rise to a self-supporting and worthy man, and possibly he will be
heard from in the world. Miss F. still points to him
as one of her most hopeless appearing cases and one
of her most successful reclamations. Whenever
she gets discouraged with her special class she thinks
of Joe and takes heart again.

CHAPTER IV

BACKWARD children do not present one type of mind, but many types. They do not necessarily think slowly, but sometimes think with sparkling rapidity. Their minds do not always develop slowly, but sometimes leap from stage to stage with wonderful strides. They are not always dull or stupid, but break out in unexpected flashes of wit. They are genuises in some things, fools in others. They are good and bad, cheerful and morose, excitable and apathetic, a medley of emotions, a turmoil of thoughts, an anarchy of actions. Their variety of types among the temporarily retarded escapes analysis, breaks through hard and fast classifications, defies rules and regulations, overturns mechanical systems of instruction, falsifies predictions of their development, humiliates prophets, and, best of all, banishes hopelessness regarding the outcome of any one of their lives. A few examples are given in this chapter to illustrate the attitude to be taken toward some of the commoner types. Because backwardness usually means slowness, the first is the story of a slow boy, an impatient teacher and an in-

terlocked course of study which demanded the same
toll from every child whò traveled that way.

The Slow Pupil.—Karl was a boy in a country
school. He was slow in everything. He was lagging in his movements, dragging in his speech, deliberate in his thought processes, and interminable in
acquiring new ideas. Yet his work was good when
it was completed. Given a problem to work out,
and left to himself, he would usually get it, and
when he got it it was almost always correct. In
arithmetic, therefore, he did not suffer so much. In
oral work like reading, spelling, parsing and analyzing sentences in class, in reciting of every kind, he
was wearisome. Examinations were written, so
though he hardly ever finished on time he was just
able to get through, because what he answered was
about correct. Unfortunately for Karl he had a
teacher who was a high-strung woman, who believed that good scholarship meant speed, and that
heaven and earth might pass away, but every jot and
tittle of the text-book must be fulfilled in the allotted
time. Furthermore, he was unfortunate in having
this same teacher for practically his entire school
life. She did not spare him. She let him know,
and the whole school and the whole neighborhood
know, that Karl was a stupid, dull-witted fellow,
with no brains and no prospect of ever acquiring
any. The frequency with which she said it, the way
she said it, and the conviction that she produced in
the minds of other pupils about it would have ut-

terly discouraged any other person differently constituted. But Karl, slow as the proverbial tortoise, also had the fine qualities of that humble animal. He held on, plodded through the grades with imperturbable patience, just squeezing through examinations, accompanied by the pity of his schoolmates, the disappointment of his parents and the increasing exasperation of his teacher, and finally left school followed by a sigh of relief in lieu of the usual congratulations.

He entered a machine shop in a neighboring city, and started at the same time to learn mechanical drawing at night. He was still slow, but it was in a business where accuracy counted for more than careless speed, where a mistake might cost thousands of dollars, and where absolute reliability, coupled with unconquerable tenacity, was sure to overcome obstacles and make success. Karl had the qualities. In both shop work and mechanical drawing he forged surely ahead. His drawing plates were models of neatness and exactness. His initial impetus to self-confidence came in his winning the medal in the night school class for the best drawing of the season. He learned his trade, gradually gravitated to the tool room where the dies for stamping metal were made, distinguished himself for his fine workmanship there, applied his mind to improving the methods of making dies and to shortening mechanical processes by means of them, and at thirty-five was at the head of that branch of work in his city, already an inventor of no mean fame, and giving promise of a greater future, the most creditable pupil his impatient teacher ever turned out of her little country school.

With the same quiet persistence he had kept up other intellectual activities, had become a splendid mathematician, a deep reader in the literature of his profession and its allied branches, and altogether one of the best versed, soundest cultured men with whom you might wish to spend a day. He had a mind strong, capable, varied in powers, but always slow moving. For such a slow but thorough mind, not quantity of practise counts, but practise taken as leisurely as it desires. Where other children might need to work ten problems to inculcate exactness, Karl needed to work but one. Had his teacher been able to diagnose his case and to fit her teachings to him, Karl would have made in actual acquisition of knowledge in a given time, as much progress as the average pupil and that knowledge would have remained with him forever.

The Concrete Mind.—The slow boy is not the only one whom the course of study and the method of teaching in the public school do not fit. Observations in many far-removed places indicate that there is a type of mind which fails ignominiously to grasp knowledge when presented in the abstract or by means of symbols, but which readily seizes upon the concrete and revels in things which the eye sees and the hands handle. Such children are often considered to be predestined to manual labor, tillers of the soil by right of birth, hewers of wood and drawers of water, shut out of the upper realms where the intellectuals who read, write and reckon, dwell. Shut out, they often are, but not so much by Providence as by a steel-riveted school-system called "common" or universal. Here is such a case from Miss Elizabeth Farrel's report from New York City. Note the cry of such a mind for its opportunity to secure an education.

This boy, fourteen years old, can not spell words like "girl," does not know how much are three times twelve; and reads second readers only. Yet his general information is fair; his attention and memory are good; and at night he reads his lessons over and over for fear of his father and teachers who "think he is lazy and unwilling to learn." While fourteen winters and summers have built up this boy's body to its height and weight, his intellect is equal to that of a seven-year-old child.

But when he is freed from purely intellectual matters and turns to manual work the miracle is wrought. All his physical training is good, at school the teachers have him doing all sorts of work.. He is especially interested in electrical apparatus and keeps all the electrical bells in repair at home. One summer he wanted a bicycle and wanted it as only a boy can want a thing. He managed to unearth two old bicycles and proposed to make one good one out of them. In spite of as-

surances from wiser heads that it could not be done,
he went right ahead, took apart, made over, re-ar-
ranged, planned and perspired until he had accomplished his purpose and rode his contraption about
the country roads as happy as a millionaire in a
touring car.

His disposition is good, but with home, school
and society against him, it is growing worse.
Under the criticism he receives he is gradually sink-
ing. He does not play naturally, he tends to spend
his time alone; his shyness, timidity, feeling of
inadequacy and doubt are slowly building around
him the prison walls of failure within which he
will be confined a morose and solitary soul. Such
would be the inevitable outcome under ordinary
circumstances; but it will not be the end here, because there is a special class and a teacher who
understands this cry of his: "I don't know why
I can't get on at school; I can't spell nor write nor
do arithmetic. I can do any sort of hand-work;
I seem to understand that by nature, but I can't
carry anything in my mind. I mean I can't see a
thing in the shop window and go home and make
any part of the toy or machine by having just seen
it in the shop. I want to be an electrician, but
realize I must know more about books if I am to
do any good work in life. If I could get an education through my hands it would be easy."

The Salvation of Sam.—Out in the mountains
of western Pennsylvania, a great hulking boy,

large for his age of sixteen, was in his first year of
high school. He was strong and healthy, with a
frank open face, and eyes that looked the simplicity
of the mind back of them. There was nothing
unusual in his personal appearance. He would
have been taken by any casual onlooker for a typical
high-school boy with evident predilection for ath-
letics. The more thoughtful observer would have
wondered why he was sixteen and just entering
high school. The fact was that he was a retarded
boy, presenting a not very unusual type of mind
which could deal efficiently and sometimes even
originally with concrete things, but groped almost
hopelessly in semi-darkness among the abstractions
of any pure science or symbolic knowledge.

His schooling in the grades had been a long-
drawn struggle, always verging on failure. He
had fallen behind his schoolmates until he was two
years retarded. His teachers had lost heart and
hope and had promoted him from grade to grade
on his age, on half what he should have known,
and in answer to his mother's importunate prayers.
He could not handle arithmetical relations with
any facility, though he could count money readily,
could make change and could see far into problems of mensuration when illustrated with any kind
of models. He read but poorly, had no taste for
literature, spelled atrociously, learned his geography
from the maps and his hygiene from the charts,
remembered his history from what his mother read

him at home and from the pictures, and so blundered along. In grammar he could not comprehend the sense or necessity for saying "I" in some places and "me" in others, and mixed "done" and "did" hopelessly. In fact, he was not much of a talker, and when he did say anything, he used the simple and incorrect language of his home and his school companions. His handwriting was unformed and boyish and, when he wrote an original composition, he showed a remarkable dearth of ideas and simplicity of inner life in thought and feeling. In short, at sixteen years of age, in all book knowledge, Sam was a boy of eleven or twelve years with little hope of going far beyond that.

His character and conduct were all that could be desired. He was good natured, with a slow easy disposition, rather shy, and avoided company instead of seeking it. In the schoolroom he seemed to try in a dull slave-minded way to get his lessons, and on the playground he looked on while others played oftener than he himself played. After school, and during vacation, he spent much time out-of-doors. He waded the mountain streams, tramped the woods, knew the beasts and birds, which he studied with curiosity, but without system, but never hunted or killed, though he came to know intuitively their songs, cries, nesting times and hiding-places.

At home he was the same good-natured fellow, doing his few chores and taking his rebukes for his poor scholarship from his ambitious mother and more phlegmatic father with a wondering patience and virtuous humility. His home was the usual one belonging to a foreman in a small boiler shop. His father had never learned much in school, had left before he completed the grades and had slowly risen to his present position by diligent work and knowledge of his trade gained wholly by intuition and rule-of-thumb practise.

Sam's mother was the head of the family. It had long been her ambition to make something more of her only child than his father ever promised to be. Like all good mothers she thought the only road to glory lay through the well-ordered demesne of public schools. So far she had been little encouraged by Sam's progress, but her unfaltering ambition had kept him in the grades and had finally started him in high school, two years behind the usual age, generally retarded, and especially lacking in power to comprehend book knowledge.

There his reception was anything but cordial. Living as he did in a small town, the high-school teachers knew him by reputation, and were acquainted, too, with the pertinacity of Sam's mother, who was determined not to let him fail nor to remove him from school until he had secured the coveted high-school diploma. Since Sam was in nowise prepared for the ordinary work of the secondary school, since Latin, or any other language was wholly out of the question, since general retardation made the subject of English, or literature, or pure mathematics, almost hopeless tasks, they looked on the necessity of teaching him with anything but enthusiasm.

Fortunately for Sam, he and manual training entered the high school together. He had handled tools more or less at home. Very likely he would have done more of such work had his father's occupation been one that lent itself easily to home practise, or one that necessitated a work-bench and chest of tools in the cellar. But his work was confined to the shop, and by his wife's command he left his menial tasks behind him when he came home. Hence Sam's real introduction to tools and hand-work, carpenter's benches, lathes, anvils, forges, and all the practicalities of the new education came in the high school. It was a veritable entrance upon a new life. For him, things seen, things palpable and tangible which the hands handle and the muscles strained over comprised the eternal verities of existence and spoke inspiring words to his innermost soul. School, heretofore a word of stagnant meaning and a place of dead monotony, became gradually a center of vivacious interest and vital powers.

He took up the course in manual training. That relieved him from the abstract studies like languages. He responded readily to the mechanical work, loved the forge, the machine shop, and the work-bench. His interest did not cease with the school hours, but he carried his zeal for his work into his home, and, in spite of the half-hearted opposition of his mother, and with the ready acquiescence of his father, he set about arranging a workshop in the cellar, and gradually accumulated a set of tools. Inspired partly by his father's trade, and partly by his innate desire to make something that moved, he spent his evenings for many months building and assembling a small steam-engine. The parts of it came from many places and by devious routes to their ultimate destination. The machine was fearfully and wonderfully made. It was unwieldy and ill proportioned, but when it was finished, the oil lamp lighted underneath the boiler made from a cut-down kitchen range water tank, the steam finally turned on, and with sundry wheezings and sputterings, the wabbly flywheel of the engine started, Sam heaved one great sigh of relief, and for almost the first time in his life, drank in draft on draft from the full cup of success. He had made something and it would go. He had conceived an idea, imperfectly, vaguely, dimly at first, but it had unfolded as he advanced with his work, and piece by piece it had grown until what at first seemed to him but an impossible dream of the night, now stood there a concrete and animated reality. How much that poor accomplishment meant to that groping soul, how it gave him the sense of power to grip his heretofore flitting ideas, how, for the first time in his conscious life, ideas themselves became sources of great possible achievements, nobody will ever know. It must all be guessed by what accompanied and followed that steam-engine building.

In the meantime, his schooling had gone on. His manual work improved in its quality. It was not better than that of the best students, for Sam was never a brilliant pupil in anything, but it was as good as the best, and wonderfully good in comparison to his book studies. It made his teachers more lenient with him in other things. It brought the feeling of ability and acquainted him with the inspiration of success, and that again served to spur him on to harder work in other directions. Then, too, it offered him living points of contact with other studies, and in this respect, more than any other study, mechanical drawing served him best. It stood for him at the center of the intricate web of knowledge, from which in one direction his mind went out readily to his beloved mechanical operations, and in the other, felt its way with increasing certainty through the dawning twilight of abstract knowledge. The kernel of the matter was contained in the process of forming and elaborating an idea, then rendering that idea visible on paper, and then, by those paper directions, transforming it into a palpable, tangible thing of beauty and joy forever. It was just the process needed by a mind like Sam's, and just that process which his primary school never offered, and which his mother, in her uninformed zeal for "education," had opposed at home.

New terms came with these studies and his vocabulary grew apace. The necessity for exact legends on drawings compelled him to spell accurately. His handwriting was always fair and his lettering was especially good. Free-hand drawing came to him rapidly and easily. He began to search mechanical journals for ideas and that helped his reading, but it must be confessed that Sam never did take to literature and the school methods never helped him much there. He grew to see the use of mathematics. Fundamentals like multiplication tables became usable and time-saving devices and accordingly of increased value and interest. Plane and solid geometry acquired meanings beyond the confusing patterns of purely imaginary lines and surfaces. On the whole, he pursued his course steadily, gaining in all his studies, and developing in his mentality. No special methods were used to teach him in his classes. Possibly the rapid increase in mental power accompanying and following pubescence, corrected a disparity between his previous physical and mental development, and gave him the necessary power to seize upon his manual training and to see through the concrete to the abstract. At any rate, he did grow.

His great awakening dated from the steam-engine. That was a home affair. His great school victory came when one day toward the end of his three years' course, his teacher announced that a chair was to be built for an educational exhibit in the state capitol. The crowning piece of work was to be the back, the honor of carving which was to go to the student offering the best original design. Sam went into the competition with a fearful fluttering heart. He worked nights, feeling his way into the invisible and unknown for his design. He faltered more than once, but the designing of the old steam-engine came back to him as he toiled, and the lessons he learned with it carried him through this infinitely larger task. Probably no other boy in that class took the matter so to heart; certainly no other one toiled so hard. Possibly it was as much the marks of infinite pains as originality of design that made the judges award Sam the privilege of making the piece of honor. The report came to him with much of the old thrill experienced when his crazy engine started, but accompanied with a humility and self-control not then known. The carving was yet to be done, but it was carried on with all the painstaking care of an artist engaged upon an altar piece, and when it was finished, it was a credit to the school. Some months later Sam stood in the capitol, saw with his own eyes the very work of his hands, looking strange and yet familiar as it stood on its platform, and experienced the rare pleasure-pain of hearing a work praised of which he knew the defects as only the man who wrought the work could possibly know them.

He was graduated with his class. He did not win any honors. He was not on the commencement program, but he probably learned more in four years than any other student in the class. His mother was as happy as any woman there that night. Then Sam went to work in the drafting room of the shop in which his father worked.

He worked hard and was advanced rapidly. To-day he is a designer of machinery in a large manufactory, holding a responsible position and sure of advancement. He is devoted to his work, faithful, enthusiastic, untiring, inventive, still a little uncertain of his grammar, not talkative nor given much to society, but he is a strong man in his profession and may some day reach the top.

When one stops and thinks what he might have been had he been continuously forced to grapple with the abstract problems of the ordinary high-school course based upon literature, languages, pure mathematics and pure sciences, until he either failed ignominiously or had rebelled against further schooling and gone out into the world untrained in anything, and fit only for the least skilled labor, without a sense of success, and with the habit of failure, then the real magnitude of his development can be measured.

Backward Because Not Interested in Lessons. —Few children in the world wholly lack interest.

They are always interested in a few things and usually interested in many things. In fact, their fault lies in the large number and the lightning-like changes of their interests rather than in the fewness of them. Hence, we frequently blame them because their attention, unlike that of grown people, is not subdued to a durable and lasting concentration on one or two subjects, and modified by experience to a mildness that does not interfere with good judgment. Sometimes, however, a child does display an attention similar to that of a specialist. In that case the child gets no credit for the display, but immediately becomes the object of most solicitous attention and urgent treatment. Especially is this true where the interest is wholly consumed on matters not pertaining to lessons, or to those activities common to other children, or to society. As a result of the child's narrow interest, he will attend to only a few activities and neglect others. Retardation in the larger affairs of life and in school is the inevitable result. This may be much or little depending upon the degree of attention remaining for those things we call lessons. In some cases the lack of attention appears to be absolutely pathological. All such instances, however, must not be taken to indicate hopeless mental retardation for life, as I shall try to show in the following example.

Katie, let us call her, was a little girl who spent the first nine years of her life without sisters or brothers, or playmates. When other girls of her age were in school in the third or fourth grades, she was at home in a room, sitting all day alone talking to herself in a very limited vocabulary, playing with the ragged dolls of her own simple manufacture, eating rudely and crudely her meals by herself, since her lack of manners forbade her eating with grown people, speaking to others almost never, and answering when spoken to only in monosyllables, signs, or meaningless grunts. She needed constant attention; she could not be permitted to go much out-of-doors; she could not play at all with other children. In short, all who knew her thought her to be an idiot, or an imbecile at best, without much mind and without hope of ever arriving at any but the simplest lessons of life. Such was Katie at nine years of age.

Then her parents heard of some children similar to her who had been wonderfully helped by special training and she was taken to a clinic. There the psychologist examined her carefully and found nothing in her family history or her own life to substantiate genuine feeble-mindedness. Diphtheria in her early childhood had caused some retardation of her growth and activities, and this, combined with her subsequent loneliness and neglect, had prevented her mind from expanding as it should have done. Her physical condition was fair; she had no special defects of the senses; she ate, slept, played in her own way. But she did not pay attention to lessons, people, or things; she seemed to have no interest; there appeared no way to arouse her dormant faculties to any realization of the daily events about her; she lacked the curiosity, the desire for novelty, and the enthusiasm of normal children.

While not positively bad or unruly in any way except one, she was immune to the effects of all the usual punishments and rewards to arouse her to an interest in duties and studies usual to the average child. Her parents had tried in their way but had failed. The father was a busy man, away from home much of the time, and the mother was a frail delicate woman who did not possess the health or the energy to do what was necessary to train so strange a child. Katie had been left largely in the hands of nurses in her babyhood and largely to herself in her childhood. Much of this neglect was also due to her terrible temper. If any attempt was made to force her to some task or to prevent her from doing the few simple things she liked to do, she first paid no attention, then grew sullen, then broke out into a paroxysm of anger, ending by crying, screaming, scratching, kicking and biting. Nothing would stop the attack except letting her alone, and that her mother and nurse had learned to do. Under these conditions, lacking, as she did, those springs within herself which force normal children to explore the world in which they find themselves, this child had lived a strange isolated existence, shut up in the fancies of her own mind, knowing little and caring less for the great world

of interests that fills the lives of others. To the
innumerable marvels of this world she was insen-
sible. She was psychically blind, deaf, dumb, almost
without human emotions, desires, thoughts or vo-
litions.

On the advice of the specialist a teacher was
secured. This woman came to live in the home.
She began with a quiet study of her strange charge.
She found that Katie, though almost absolutely
destitute of interests, did have a few. While most
of the time during the day she sat, wide-eyed and
wondering, with mind apparently blank, or mut-
tered words to herself, at other times, she repeated
over and over again rhythmic syllables without
meaning and with little tune, but in a sing-song
manner. That was a clue to the teacher. When
Katie "tra-la-la-ed," the teacher did the same and
they both fell into unison. Katie seemed to enjoy
it. She kept up the exercise longer than when she
did it alone. Next, the teacher noted if she began
it first and kept it up for a little while, Katie would
also begin the rhythm.

The next stage came when the little girl showed
by unmistakable signs that she was actually enjoy-
ing the fun; and the next when she made it known
by pulling the teacher's hand, grunting that she
wanted her teacher to "sing" with her. It was easy
to fix a sign to this desire and Katie learned the
"ting" and learned to iterate it, with sundry other
signs, until the teacher would start the tune. From

those simple beginnings came the whole after-training of the little girl who seemed at first so hopeless.

A piano was added to the equipment and the teacher drummed upon it the rhythmic scale they had been singing. At first the music fell upon dead ears. Gradually, however, the strange girl whose only interest was in rhythm, began to note the sound and to fall into harmony with it until, as in her previous accompaniment of her teacher's voice, she likewise learned to follow the piano. That was a great event and the teacher's joy in it was faintly shared by the groping mind beginning to taste for the first time the pleasure of attainment. From notes and snatches of melody, more or less disconnected, they went on to little songs. Words were added, albeit slowly and laboriously, until Katie's monotonous life became comparatively rich and variegated in its new activities.

Along with the singing and music Katie learned to beat time; first with her hands and then with her feet. Very soon, for she began to show a genius for such things, she proceeded to dancing; and with that came a whole flood of health-giving and developing exercises. Then her teacher ventured to take her to a theater where dancing occupied a large part in the performance. In the life of this little hermit that day was a pilgrimage to a promised land. She came home burning with a new ambition. She was wild to imitate what she had seen. She practised her dancing with all her might and learned it rapidly. Theater-going became a part of her education; its sights and sounds were the stimulators of her endeavors and the rewards of her achievements; the stage was the goal of her ambition.

One day she thought of the clothes those splendid people on the stage wore. She wanted dresses like them. Her wise teacher saw another opportunity and proposed that they make the dresses themselves. That introduced into the curriculum all the mysteries and discipline of sewing. How that proceeded, first painfully and laboriously, but finally triumphantly, I must let the teacher who has taught it imagine. When Katie, arrayed in one of her own creations, preened herself before the mirror, which had been brought into her room, and then pirouetted across the room like the great ladies of the stage world, she did it with all the abandon of a normal child dressed in her mother's skirts.

From dancing and costuming, it was only a step to acting, to repeating dialogues, at first elementary, incoherent and sketchy; from dialogues to recitations, committed to memory with rapidly increasing power under the stimulation of great and enthusiastic interest. Under such tuition, Katie's mind grew like a long-delayed plant taken from the cellar and set in the sun. Her power of concentration grew daily and her memory with it; her vocabulary multiplied itself; her increasing powers of acquisition naturally led her on to continually more ambitious tasks, and keen enjoyment of her new-found varieties of self-expression spurred her to continuous effort. The balance maintained between the exercise contained in dancing and sewing and the mental activity found in memorizing and reciting, saved her from any untoward effects which she might have suffered from a too rapid mental growth.

Her teacher had wisely left her moral training in the background. Her temper had been the chief obstacle to any education that her mother might have given her. Coercion of any kind, as I have already said, had always thrown her into tantrums, which ended in complete collapses for her mother and nervous spasms for herself. Though the frequency of such outbreaks had continually diminished with the multiplication of her interests, they still remained, and on occasions, Katie showed with due fierceness her old-time paroxysms. She soon found, however, that her steady-nerved teacher did not collapse and give up. She was told also that whenever she gave way to such tempers she would not be taken to the beloved theater, and found that when such an edict went forth, it was irrevocable. Though she screamed, stamped, danced and threw herself on the floor and kicked, it was energy wasted, and the little lady gradually learned the great moral lesson of obedience. On the other hand, she found that docility and diligent application to lessons and tasks always met with their deserved rewards. Therefore she soon fell into doing what was told her and not doing what was forbidden her.

To this training was added the stimulation of great examples. She worshiped the heroines and heroes of the stage. When she was arrayed in her home-made finery, her lively imagination and power of mimicry transformed her in her own mind into something very closely akin, if not identical, with these demigods. Of course, she expected some day to become one of them really and truly. "If that is so," said her teacher, "then you must be like them all the time. You must be patient, courteous, kind, noble and queenly, just as those people are." And Katie tried with all her might.

From love of music she came to playing music. At first she played by ear. Then she undertook regular music lessons and learned a new meaning and extracted an unlimited pleasure from the peculiar black-knobbed signs on the music sheets. It was not very long before she mastered the simplest music. Then her attention reached out to the other symbols in black that ran between the notes and from which her teacher taught her the words of songs. Could she learn those, too? Certainly. And so reading began and went on rapidly. Then the reading of simple plays followed, and almost before Katie knew it she was ushered into another world of great characters in fiction.

All this time, the other activities of her life were

cared for. Her exercises grew out of her dancing.
Once the pleasure of movement was tasted, it could
not be confined to one variety. The usual children's exercises—jumping the rope, running,
swinging clubs and dumb-bells—came into play.
Health and strength increased aboundingly. Games
followed; then playmates came in and took part and
along with them came all the world of self-control
and unselfishness and the awakening of friendship
and love. Sewing and the piano practise gave first
manual lessons. They were continued in dressing,
washing, eating and all the amenities of polite life,
all of them inspired by the ambition to become like
the personages of the stage or the novel.

From musical notes and letters in song and
drama, Katie passed to other studies, and mastered
them fairly well for one so long retarded. The
weary steps she took in a few years, the hours of
labor, the lapses she suffered in intellectual and
moral training, the patience required by her teacher,
I shall pass over. They were there and they were
discouraging enough. In all of them the firm and
skilful trainer supplied the will that poor Katie
lacked and without which her life would in all
probability have continued enclosed to the end in
the psychic prison in which it began. In about three
years the little girl who at nine was counted an
imbecile had developed so marvelously that she
could take her part in any company of twelve-year-
old children, and could comport herself with the

manners of a proper child in any society. She was an inveterate and earnest reader, possessed a comparatively rich and varied command of language and an expressed ambition "to add at least one new word to her vocabulary every day."

Katie's case is interesting from many points of view. It is such an extreme one that teachers never expect to see one like it in school, and parents feel it to be utterly unthinkable to have one like it in their home. Yet at bottom, Katie's difficulty might be exemplified in milder form in numberless instances. Notice, she was not mentally abnormal. She was not dull, nor stupid, nor slow. She was not a "born criminal," nor a moral imbecile, nor a degenerate fallen from higher moral planes. She had no bad family history, nor any diseases in her own lifetime which left indelible marks. Katie was merely the victim of extreme bad management. The core of all her later troubles lay in her lack of those varied interests which compel ordinary children to educate themselves. All her evils developed when unskilled adults, without a study of her condition, undertook to force her into the usual molds of training. She was made of stubborn metal, tough, fine-grained, high-tempered, and the molds broke. Then came a seer who perceived the germ of her mental life, treated Katie as if she was a living organism and a human being, fitted instruction to pupil, saved a soul from mental torture and formed a noble woman out of a potential maniac.

CHAPTER V

BAD AND BACKWARD

BACKWARDNESS and badness are sometimes related as cause to effect. A boy is backward because he is bad. This happens in school where conduct counts so much for advancement that sometimes amiable feeble-minded children are promoted from grade to grade with praise for their splendid behavior and for their evident sincere attempts to study, while pupils really bright are held back in their grades and counted mentally retarded because they are unruly. No teacher, of course, deliberately plans such anomalies of educational practise. But for that very reason, because such unintended results sometimes follow, we should study the matter. The following case illustrates some of the evils arising from treating bad bright boys as if they were mentally retarded.

George was brought to the clinic by his mother because his school said he was a backward boy. He did not look it, nor did he in his appearance live up to the stories told about him and the confessions he later made. It was a curious confusion due to opposite view-points, and a natural confusion of opinions that was presented by the teachers and his mother. But first let us have a look at the boy.

He was about twelve years of age; well dressed, clean, red-cheeked, slightly freckled through his tanned skin. The tan argued that he was much out-of-doors; for it is unusual, even in summer, for a city boy to secure such a healthy coat of brown. He was a manly-looking fellow, strong and well, with broad shoulders, a quiet, somewhat suppressed manner which spoke as much for self-control as it did for discipline, as much for a hidden life as it did training in manners. In his own history there was not a sign of abnormality. Neither was there an item in his family history that could be construed as moral or mental deficiency. All this was borne out also by his mother's general appearance and by her evident character and ability. She was a widow engaged in some easy and lucrative work befitting her capacity, so that George suffered neither the hardships nor the privations of an orphaned boy, except that his mother was forced to be away from home during the day, and he lacked the sympathetic understanding and the guidance of a father when he needed them most.

The history of his schooling was altogether of a different color. At six years of age George had started to the regular public school in a large eastern city. From the beginning he did well and for three years gave absolutely no trouble, learning his lessons like a worthy pupil, securing good grades and be-

having like a little gentleman. Then for some un-
explained reason, in one of those educational re-
arrangements common to growing neighborhoods,
George found himself compelled to go to another
public school in quite another neighborhood. It
was not such a great distance from his home, but
it was in a neighborhood infinitely removed from
his in social conditions. From boys of his own
class he passed to boys of an altogether different
class: children from the slums, whites and blacks,
whose homes and no-account parents made them
what they were, objects of pity rather than objects
of censure, but little demons, nevertheless, potent
with influences and powers to make others like
themselves.

The new boy had his troubles from the first.
He was a stranger and therefore a suspicious character. After the first flush of antagonism because
of his strangeness had worn off his evident social
superiority, his good-breeding and his scholarship,
made him a natural enemy to the hoodlum element.
Like all strange boys in that school he had to fight
his way. That he could do with right good gusto.
George was no weakling; he was not a coward, nor
was he sickly, nor had he any squeamish ethical
ideas that unfitted him for the robustious world of
boys into which he had been thrown. His training
on the streets had not refined away any of his
natural Irish belligerency, nor imbued him with any
notions of passive resistance. Likewise he had a

just estimate of his superior social position and
made no concealment of the fact that he considered
his removal from the other school unjust and his
association with these new companions a degrada-
tion.   Naturally he had to fight for such ideals;
and fight he did with the necessary frequency and
the necessary vigor.   As a result he both gained
and lost.   He made himself a solid place in the boy-
world where he was respected and where he ruled
with a good-natured despotism.   For it must be
said to his credit that he never picked a quarrel and
he never fought unless he thought he had to do so
for some principle, or for some end to be gained.
Of course, the tales of his fighting reached the
teachers.   He was reprimanded and punished.   He
went through all the formalities to which a boy is
subjected by a machine that attempts to force the
standards of civilized and cultured life upon a barbarian society.   His teachers lectured him on the
ungentlemanliness of fighting with bad boys, appealed to his evident superior breeding, besought
him in his mother's name, scolded, kept him after
school, wrote notes to his mother, gave him marks
of demerit, cut down his grades, threatened to send
him to the school for incorrigibles, and finally, in
despair, themselves descended to his plane, and
seizing the rod of superior physical prowess proceeded with exactly the same tactics that George
found he had been compelled to pursue on the play-

ground. Through it all, the teachers felt doubly outraged because they believed that the boy was bright and could settle down and study in peace and quiet if he only would do it. However, his study continued to suffer and his reputation for pugnacity grew. It is an open question whether George did not find more compensation from the knowledge of supremacy in his own world than he lost from the feeling of failure in the school-world. He had entered the first stages of the real hoodlum.

His principal, at last worn out with attempts to reform George, sent him to a school for the incorrigibles. There he was to stay until he worked his way out by a system of credits whereby every day's good conduct was rewarded with a ticket, thirty of which released the young prisoner from his ignominious incarceration. If his former school was a school of pugnacity the second was infinitely worse. Here the lowest boys of many neighborhoods were corralled; pugnacity was concentrated; truancy was incarnated and walked abroad in visible heroes who would "bag" school in the face of certain death; burglars in embryo, pickpockets in the tutelage, gamblers in reality, braggadocios in petty criminality, heroes of juvenile courts and houses of detention, stalked about like kings with their followers, many of whom were feeble-minded and all of whom were in that impressionable and suggestible stage where daredevil misdemeanors lent to the perpetrator a glamour beside which the halo of a saint flickered and went out like a candle in the Valley of Death.

So at least it looked to George and the other boys, according to his story to the clinic staff. Fortunately George was too bright and too well-bred to be caught with the tinsel of cheap viciousness and the showy exhibition of vulgar vainglory. The whole thing bored him. All he wanted was to be let alone. That peace was impossible to be had except by fighting for it. "Why didn't you work your way out by merits?" George was asked. "I did try," he answered wearily, "but the other fellows wouldn't leave me alone. Once I got twenty-nine tickets and then I had to lick a fellow that got fresh, and they took all my tickets away again."

It was hard for the clinic staff to believe that this clean-cut chap, who ought by all odds to have been a good scholar in a regular school, had been kept in a place like that for causes like that for nearly two years, but his mother corroborated the story and later it was found to be true by the clinic social worker.

The opinion of George's mother varied essentially from the lurid reputation he had acquired at school. She insisted that he was a good boy; that he was gentlemanly in his conduct, obedient at home, regular in his habits and diligent in his attempts to get his lessons. When asked how he spent his evenings, she affirmed that he usually spent them at home, but he went out sometimes, and once a week with her permission, attended the moving-picture show. All his troubles at school she blamed on the principal, who, she averred, had taken a violent dislike to her son, and had maliciously kept him in a school for incorrigibles for a period beyond all justice or reason. It might be said in passing that George did not entirely deserve this angelic opinion of his mother and he admitted that he frequently slipped out at night and got into the moving-picture show by doing odd jobs for the manager. I believe, too, he admitted to a recently acquired taste for cigarettes. If he did not smoke and swear he must have been born a saint.

Such was the situation. Undoubtedly George was not retarded because of any mental deficiency. His trouble was badness; or, to be more correct and specific,—fighting. From all appearances his fighting was forced on him by circumstances. Like primitive man, he knew no other mode of settling his difficulties in the society where he had fallen through no fault of his own. When this conclusion was reached, friends laid the matter before the superintendent of schools who cut some red tape and speedily removed George to his old school where he first started. There George settled down again to study, left off fighting more than the usual amount necessary to boys and conducive to order in their world, and at last accounts was making up lost ground.

A Hopeless Case.—Admit it we must: some children are born bad and they can not be cured of their badness. This fact, unbelievable to some people, and not discerned in individual cases by others, has led and continues to lead to many complications and much confusion regarding the moral training of children. Theories are laid down by traditions or by inventors, methods are elaborated to fit them, and all comes to naught because the child was not carefully studied and his true condition ascertained before any effort was made to cure him. Some mental defect always accompanies true moral imbecility. With the clinics for children well organized, as they are to-day, guesswork is not necessary. That it will be continued for some time to come is a prophecy in line with all history. It takes time for new knowledge to escape from the confines of laboratories and to penetrate the practises of the crowd. The following illustration shows many things; chief among them is the fact that moral imbecility exists, that scientists can diagnose it, and that long and costly experimentation brings the doubters to the same conclusion.

Rose was a girl about eleven years old when she came to a clinic. She was a well-formed beautiful child, with a face in which the hint of voluptuousness was chastened into cherubic purity by the innocence of childhood; with eyes that were full and deep as the sky in June, and as untarnished as a violet by the spring, with hair that fell in long chestnut curls, crisp and shimmering in its wealth and health. Her teeth were large and white and her charming smile unveiled them frankly with an inviting trust and wholesome good-humor. Her skin was clear and clean, a surprising fact considering that she came from a very poor family. She suffered from adenoids, enlarged tonsils and a slight defect of vision. She was brought to a clinic because she was expelled from school for general misbehavior. She spent her time while away from school on the streets and in the alleys, playing and fighting, stealing rides on wagons and fleeing the police. Her home was poor in all its aspects, physical, mental and moral. The less said about the family the better. Sufficient will it be to remark that while there were no marked mental or moral abnormalities in her family, all of her immediate relatives were worthless or nearly so. There were some positive immoralities, but they were of the weak kind, arguing for no character, not bad character. All of her relatives, her mother, father, sisters and brothers, might have been summarized in that most significant southern phrase, "poor white trash." To the clinicist, this was the most damaging testimony in the whole case.

Rose exhibited a similar weakness in mental capacities. She was not distinctly feeble-minded, but she was fearfully retarded for no reason except irregular attendance at school and her inability to learn when she was there. She was twelve years of age and in the second grade, and not up to that grade in some studies. Poor heredity and bad environment had cooperated all through her life, and before her life, to make her an exceedingly bad and backward child, though fair and beautiful to look upon. The impartial clinicist pronounced his verdict according to the evidence, that it was useless to try to keep her in society, and advised that she be sent to some institution where she would be protected from herself and prevented from doing the damage to society that she would not fail to do if she were permitted to go at large. However, Rose had succeeded by her charms in touching the heart of a very splendid young woman who gave herself without stint to aiding unfortunate children anywhere and everywhere. This good-hearted girl deemed the results of the examination too harsh and hard and made up her mind to give Rose another chance.

She secured the child's admission to an institution for children in the country where Rose for the first time in her life entered a healthy and pleasant home. As a result of the novelty, her conduct for two weeks was reported as good in every way. Then she went back to her own home again. Her conduct soon reverted to its former evil state. Her playground was the street, and her conduct so disorderly that the police again interfered and threatened her with arrest. Her friend secured her a boarding-place in the country where her actions were soon reported to be unbearable. Then she went to a children's hospital for an operation and treatment, whence, as soon as her treatment was concluded, she was removed by request because of her badness. Her friend, still stanch in her efforts to save so beautiful a child, took her into her own home. But it was of no avail. Kindness went for naught; it was answered by impertinence, disobedience, blasphemy and vileness. Back she went to a caretaker in a special home. For five weeks she stayed there and then her friend took her for a vacation to the seashore. There she was ill and fairly good for a while, but not good enough to show any real development in morality. Her benefactress was becoming discouraged and tried her next in a colony for delinquent children. There she was disobedient, quarrelsome, used improper and vile language and exhibited a marked and vicious propensity for boys' society. That was the last attempt to reform her. The doors of a house of refuge in which there is practically no hope closed upon her and she is there now. Six institutions, five doctors and a host of friends, none more loyal and patient to be found than Rose's benefactress, had tried their utmost for a year and a half and had not made the slightest progress in developing a moral nature in the girl.

Her immorality was due to heredity and environment. Her home was poor, her neighborhood bad, the effect of her surroundings augmented by physical defects. Although attractive in personal appearance and promising in character, she was devoid of moral sense, and impervious to elevating surroundings or elevating ideals. This brief sketch gives but a faint idea of her depravity, her vileness, her degenerate tastes, her familiarity with certain crimes, her versatility in blasphemous language, all of it springing out of a nature that sought vice with the unchecked determination of an animal following its instincts. Yet she was as beautiful as an angel, as sweet as a little child.

A Pseudo-Moral Imbecile.—To show, however, that children may be saved who exhibit on the surface all the characteristics and worse ones than those just enumerated in Rose's life, let me give a brief résumé of another case leading to an altogether different conclusion. In *The Psychological Clinic*, Miss Catlin gives an interesting and detailed account of her experiences with a girl who was entrusted to her care for about two years. The child's mother died in childbirth and the baby was thrown upon the care of nurses and others. At eight she was a terror to all who knew her. Her health, undermined by indulgences of many kinds, was precarious, her temper frightful, her nature soured and warped, her resentment at interference fierce and lasting. Her face wore a wolfish aspect that made her more animal than human in appearance. The family, utterly despairing of doing anything with her, sent her to a special trainer.

There for two years she was compelled to lead a physically well-ordered, hygienic life, with the result that her health improved greatly but her disposition remained about the same. Her teacher, when handing the child over to Miss Catlin, reported that she was still ungovernable, that she was absolutely wanting in "decency, honesty, truth; was cruel, sneaky, filthy," and concluded with the firm conviction that the child was insane and should be examined by an alienist. In spite of this Miss Catlin received her into her care and trained her for two years.

She began with her own diagnosis of the case. She took account of stock and reckoned up the moral assets and liabilities with which she was to begin business. She found that all the evil told of the child was true; in fact that half had not been told. To all her other evils she added the art of tormenting people out of their wits. She knew how because she possessed a bright mind sharpened to a keenness almost uncanny by her ten years of constant warfare against her enemies whom she hated with the hatred of a savage and whom she loved to out-do by any sort of cunning and to hurt by any exquisite torture. Her new teacher soon discovered another fault which she immediately set down as an asset. That was vanity growing out of an all-pervading egotism. Her one real streak of gold was sympathy which Sarai, let us call her, possessed to a marked degree, but which seemingly had never been discovered before and certainly had not been developed. This quality of sympathy determined the teacher in her choice of the mode of training to be followed with this problematical child.

Immediately she made herself a chum to her charge, adopting even the same kind of dress. For a month both ran wild on an isolated farm. During that time Miss Catlin made herself absolutely indispensable to her pupil so that even if she were away for an hour the girl felt it keenly. For the first two weeks the little demon tried by every diabolical art, like dropping caterpillars down her teacher's back, jumping at her from corners, and dangling snakes within an inch from her nose, to test the staying powers of her new friend's good humor. The first streak of dawn in the otherwise dark training up to that time, came when the teasing grew so unbearable that the teacher took to flight and showed by unmistakable signs, not the anger the little girl expected, but the awful hurt her friend was suffering through her misconduct. She timidly stole up to her teacher, took her hand and whispered, "Sister, do you feel like you look?" In that moment the teacher knew that her method was right and would eventually succeed.

Every morning there was a thought for the day. Then came the stage, most cleverly brought on, when the child gave her word for stated tasks and never broke her promise. Then the promising was generalized and she was asked to promise always to do anything she was told. By that time she had learned that her new teacher would never ask her to do anything arbitrary. Later the two further qualifications of "promptness" and "cheerfulness" were added and the lesson of obedience was completely learned. Cheerfulness was applied to more than mere obedience. It was to be carried into everything, even to the loss of games which sorely tried the little egotist's vanity. One day at tennis, Miss C. dropped her racket and said, "See here, I'm not going to play out of my class. I'm a sport! What are you? Do you know what a sport is?"

"I'm not sure," the subdued playmate said.

"Well, it's one who plays fair, and is a good loser! . . . Are you a sport?"

"I don't think I was born one," was the honest reply, "but I might grow to be one, couldn't I?" And you may be sure she received assurances concerning the prepotency of human will over heredity.

The thoughts of the morning gradually grew from ideals for a day to purposes for life. Her teacher early and energetically inculcated the notion that everybody without exception should have a work in the world and do it with a right good will. The kind old gentleman will never know what disdain and indignation he aroused by calling the girl who looks confidently forward to earning her own living a "little lady."

Her schooling after about a month of freedom began with one hour's study a day. The beginning was as sore a trial as her moral training. Her knowledge of books, and almost all else, was practically nothing. Yet she had the supremest opinion of her own intellectual attainments. She knew everything and resented warmly any imputation to the contrary. Some of her vagaries were ludicrous. When she was given "there" to write and wrote it, and immediately following that was given "then," she quite economically wrote "hen" underneath it, asserting, and quite rightly as far as that fragmentary situation went, that one "t" could stand for both. None but a bright child would have thought of that. In such instances nothing but the threat of her teacher to leave her would compel the necessary routine. With these few exceptions her lessons went on rapidly. She apparently needed no special kind of instruction for her mind was normal, but neglected. At the end of four months she went to a private school where she continued without difficulty for eight months.

At ten years she was a suspected moral imbecile with maniacal tendencies, cruel, indecent, dishonest, deceitful, tricky, filthy, incapable of living with normal people or mixing with ordinary children, a creature despised and apparently doomed to a life of horror; at twelve she was a well-bred little lady, "kindly, lovable, thoughtful, earnest, loyal," in school learning rapidly, playing with other children, sincerely ambitious to make her life useful and noble in the fullest degree. The first state, contrary to the opinion of her first teacher, was not due to mental defect nor to ungovernable passion within the child herself but to misdirected energies. The new state was brought about by the simple but laborious direction of the same fundamental energies into new and useful channels.

Laziness.—One of the commonest charges brought against backward children when the backwardness is so mild that it does not demand serious investigation, is the charge of laziness. It is an easy mode of explaining hard things. Besides, the backward child exhibits so many symptoms of laziness. In fact, a lazy boy and a "truly backward" boy, if they are not suffering from precisely the same fundamental pathological conditions, certainly act as if they were. But it is the traditional method with children to declare that they are born with depravity in them and their worth of character comes largely, if not wholly, from training. However, science in its advances encroaches more and more not only upon the realms of superstition but also upon the empires of tradition. Many hoary-headed opinions concerning children, when examined impartially, melt away like snow under the April sun. One of these is the traditional notion that because they do not like work or study, healthy, outdoor, sun-loving, young barbarians are lazy. The fact that the accusation rests chiefly against boys and not girls suggests some ground for suspicion that it is unjust.

Modern child-study has done much to explode the theory of "just pure laziness" as a cause for a boy's so-called idleness. The youthful, good-for-nothing, rat-catching Darwin, who later was amazed at his own industry displayed in reading whole masses of biological literature; a boy called "Pat," who alternated fits of extremest laziness with spells of hunting without which the orator of the Revolution might never have proclaimed to the centuries "Give me liberty or give me death"; and a host of others have done much to dispel the prophecy that "lazy" boys are sure to fail. The lifelong sufferings of Horace Mann, due largely to his work-laden boyhood, is a protest against adult-defined diligence as the proper virtue for children. Added to these admonitions comes Doctor Hutchison with his half-jocular toxin-theory of work and his warning against infection by the deadly habit of industry, on the one hand, and the hook-worm with its genuine infection of laziness on the other. Out of this medley of theories and babel of new voices, for every child trainer must come a revision of doctrine concerning the old simple formula of "He is lazy."

Possibly laziness in children really exists. If it does and is the cause of some pupils' poor progress in school, possibly the direct method of the father who gave his two boys a sound beating because their monthly grades were low, may be effective for curing the low grades. The method has in its favor at least the simplicity of brutality. If, however, it should turn out that all children called lazy are in reality suffering from perfectly definite but as yet only partially known pathological conditions, punishment would appear to be as barbarous as beating a sick savage in order to expel the evil spirit causing the disease; and if, as is now generally believed, a very large majority of cases of so-called laziness have their distinct causes, it would seem to be only rudimentary justice to study each case carefully in order to discover the cause. Finally, so-called laziness may turn out to be a man's salvation.

A couple of boys lived on a farm where both were compelled to work hard to force a living for the family out of the unwilling soil. One boy took to the work willingly. He did his chores, "plowed and sowed, bought and sold" as his forefathers had done with never a vision beyond the mechanical order of the day. The other hated the farm work, did as little as he could, would walk miles to borrow a book and then would crawl off in the haymow or some other place and pore over it all day. He was slow, inactive, dilatory in all manual occupations and received early the opprobrious title of "lazy bones." At the first opportunity he left the farm and went into the city, secured an office position in a business corporation and is to-day an influential officer in that organization. His "diligent" brother remained on the farm, "diligently" plied his trade with diminishing success, but continual labor, till the foreclosure of a mortgage threatened to alienate the homestead from the family and it was saved only by the "lazy" brother, who bought it in and now hires his "diligent" brother to farm it for him.

Such an instance does not prove that laziness does not exist, but it does go to show that laziness should be more accurately defined and each suspected case carefully diagnosed before summary action is taken. A period comes in many a high-school boy's life when rapid physical growth saps his energies; when disgust for old things begets tastes for new things; when restlessness drives and doubt guides, and the whole life eddies, then stands still and stagnates. Such a boy often falls behind in study, is charged with gross laziness, and sometimes is driven by extreme measures into acts ruinous to his whole life. For the lazy boy, young or old, I would make a plea for the most discriminating study and the most patient treatment. I have heard a successful man in middle life devoutly thank God for the profound laziness of his youth because it permitted the incubation of purposes that changed the direction of his whole career.

All of us know the evil effects of truancy on school progress. Few of us know infallibly how to cure it. Some of us believe that truants are born and truants are made. The former truants must have their fling for a time at least; must learn the bitter truth little Hugh Idle learned who ran away from Mr. Toil, his hated schoolmaster, fell in with a most congenial traveler along the road, stopped with him to admire one interesting activity after another always to be frightened half out of his wits by seeing one of Mr. Toil's everlasting brothers energetically bossing the job. Night came at last, and poor Hugh turned to his fellow-traveler with the tearful question, "Is there nothing but Toil in the world?" to discover to his utter dismay that he had been in the company of Toil all day long. That is one of the fables in our school readers, one of the lessons we do not learn while young, but do learn when we are older, by experience and only by experience, and then forget that lesson the moment we ourselves begin to deal with the faults of children. Verily, I do believe that born-truants must have the truancy taken out of them by the long and dusty road, by the hardships of ignorance, by the labor inevitably involved in fleeing from toil. The wise rich father sends his truant son on a long voyage with one of his captains; or his son falls overboard, as Kipling's hero did, and tastes the bitterness of ignorance upon a fishing-smack. Poor men's sons can not always do that and sometimes they end tragically because they can not, as the sequel to the following story will show.

A Truant Made.—When I first saw Ikey he was in a special summer school, and I did not wonder that a teacher had taken the trouble to travel half-way across the city to warn the lady in charge against the little rogue. She described his ignorance, his stupidity, his unruliness, his truancy, his deceitfulness, his constant aggravation of his mental ills by most persistent moral turpitude. She, for one, was convinced that he was a moral degenerate and mentally unsound, and that further efforts on his behalf would be worse than useless because they would do no good to Ikey and he would do untold harm to the other summer-school pupils.

And Ikey looked it. He was undersized in body and limb; with a queer, little, wizened face, scarred by old burns that affected one eye and gave an odd and impish quirk to his grin. His hair was cut *a la Pompadour,* and stood up over his low forehead like the spines of a hedgehog. His clothes betokened his lowly condition; they were ragged and dirty; his shoes, old button-shoes, were run down at the heel, full of holes and half the buttons were gone. He was a typical slum child, a "wharf-rat," with all the cunning of the species written in every line of his face, every thread of his clothes, in the ready poise and in every startled, scuttling movement of his body. His beady eyes glistened and danced, a flat denial to the charge of stupidity. The tentative, twisted uncovering of his crooked teeth offered either enmity or friendship, and according to the exigencies of the occasion, might turn into a snarl or a smile. One could not associate a loud, hearty laugh with Ikey. A silent series of chuckles is as much as one could expect under the most mirthful circumstances.

Into his home and schooling we need not go. Both can better be imagined than described. We can

begin our admiration for Ikey by noting that neither
home nor school had broken his spring-steel spirit,
though between them they had put kinks in it. Fortunately for the waif of a city's wreckage, he had
fallen at last into the hands of Miss F., the same
teacher who dealt with Joe described in Chapter I.
She had a habit of looking through the outside of
teachers and boys and things, and so after glancing
at the hat of the teacher who pursued Ikey across
the city, she courteously dismissed the prophet and
the prophecy of evil and turned to the boy. She
saw all I have described, and likely she saw more.
Anyhow, from Ikey's facial contortions emerged
a confessed smile and his schooling began.

And now when our story should reach its climax
of interest in the pedagogical struggle that ought
to follow, we really have little to say. The battle
was all won when this kind of a special class was organized and a teacher like Miss F. was born. The
very novelty held the truant for about a week. It
was all so strange. Class began with all the fifteen
pupils arranged about the teacher as they do in a
kindergarten, and then they all told what they
wanted to do during the day and how they would
do it. After that each went to the board and wrote
what he would do; then he read it and had it corrected; then he went and did it. The "it" consisted
of something different for each child and included
manual work of all kinds; reading, writing, arithmetic, games, a lunch with *ice-cream,* a nap, a swim,

a walk in the park, and a lingering farewell at four
o'clock. No wonder a boy like poor street-hardened
Ikey counted it all a paradise, never missed a day,
rain or shine, though he walked six miles a day, and
at the end of the summer came to the principal's office and begged to be permitted to come back to that
school next year. He studied, too, and did well for
him, considering his previous disadvantages. He
certainly was not an imbecile, neither a degenerate,
neither an incorrigible, but just a little cobble-stone,
kicked loose from the streets where travel had worn
him hard and smooth. At the end of six weeks the
great city opened its maw and swallowed him again,
and I have not seen him since. Often I have wanted
to hear how he turned out and have hoped against
hope that he did well. At least, it was demonstrated that he was a truant made and not a truant
born.

A Truant Born.—Bert was a truant born. At
thirteen he bore about with him the air of a rover
and the *ennui* of a man of the world. I met him
in the same summer-school with Ikey. They were
altogether different. Bert was large, well-formed,
easy-mannered, hated to be in a class with "kids"
and boarded at a place where some of them "cried
at night to go home!" That to him was the nether-
most depth of imbecile puerility. He never wanted
to go home. In fact, for several years he had been
using every effort to get away from home to go west
and lead a wild untrammeled life on a ranch. He

had started on his free-life career via truancy, but it had ended so far rather humiliatingly. He had been sent to a truant school, been in the juvenile court, in the detention house, on probation, in a protectory, and between times, frequently in the hands of the police. Through it all his study naturally suffered, and at thirteen he was having a new trial in a summer class for backward children. There he was making a good impression by his lazy smile, his drawling tones, his ready ability and unfailing politeness. The matron with whom he boarded said he had a "good face" and was the most "gentlemanly boy she ever saw." When he obligingly offered to take a ten-dollar check to the store and get it cashed for her she readily signed it and telephoned the store to give him the money.

When Bert was next heard of he was in a soldiers' camp in another state. He had taken the ten dollars, equipped himself with a brand new khaki uniform, taken a train, passed through the largest city in America, changed from train to boat, from boat to trolley-car, thence to train again, with the unerring scent of a pointer-dog winding a covey of partridges, and arrived at the soldiers' camp only to find his expected friend was not there. Nothing abashed, he soon made friends, was boarded and petted, and finally wrote a post-card to his father admonishing him not to worry. Before the police came he was on his way home, and arrived in his native city with twenty-five cents, with which, like a true man of the world, he took one last fling at an amusement park. Then he reported at the police station that he was a lost boy and "wouldn't they take him home?" Which they did in the patrol-wagon, and nothing was lacking in Bert's arrival save a band playing "See, the Conquering Hero Comes."

Poor Bert! That was about his last escapade. All the threats and punishments could not cure his craving for the West. His parents thought they could cure it, or, to be more accurate, they did not think at all, and following in their poor blind way the traditions of society, attempted by paternal authority and organized social machinery to suppress the vagrancy of their unguided boy. But in spite of it all, Bert slipped through the meshes, took a freight-train for his promised land, fell under the wheels and his restless spirit free forever, winged away on its last long journey.

In the face of such tragedy, pedagogy feels the propriety of silent reflection. Yet for the sake of other parents with other boys, I must add my firm conviction that Bert might have been saved and cured from his truancy. Purposefully, I have brought together Ikey and Bert in order to show from the first how the second might have been helped, and to show from the second how serious it is to attempt to suppress the vagrant impulses of boys when they are manifested so persistently and so strenuously. I believe that if Bert's parents had

arranged for him to go west and by the toil and
sweat of actual cowboy life, to work out of his system the romance and glamour surrounding his notion of ranch life, he would have come to himself
and would have returned a chastened and wiser
youth. He had brains and ability, he was not irra-
tionally bad, he was not a general vagrant nor
merely an aimless truant, but he was a boy with a
fixed obsession, and the lure of that obsession led
him to his death. If we dare generalize from these
cases, and others like them, I would say that truancy is nearly always due to environment, and if
taken in time, can be cured by the proper modifica-
tion of the school conditions.

CHAPTER VI

RETARDATION DUE TO ENVIRONMENT

THE causes of mental retardation are resident either within the child himself or outside of him. Since the retardation is so often discovered in school where the first exact methods of classifying children are applied, it frequently happens that the causes for the retardation are looked for in the school. Parents say the curriculum is too crowded or too difficult, the lessons too long, the text-books incomprehensible, the teacher unfit, the method of teaching outworn or experimental. It is seldom that the school-administrator has a chance to make an adequate reply and so the charges stand.

The fact is that causes for retardation very often lie in the child's home, or in his neighborhood, or in the kinds of companions he keeps. Sometimes the causes are physical; sometimes they are due to the ideals he imbibes.

Because of their exceeding triviality, the causes are frequently overlooked. So serious does pedagogical retardation appear to the average school-administrator that he is misled into thinking that a serious cause must surely lie at the bottom of so

110

serious a condition. He therefore looks for deep-seated defects in the pupil's physical or mental being, or for sinister influences in his surroundings, when, as a matter of fact, frequently the cause is so trivial and superficial that he overlooks it. Causes that are ludicrous except for the gravity of their effect, and too ridiculous to be set down except for their frequency, will readily occur to any seasoned teacher. Partly to warn teachers, in cases of retardation, to look first for the obvious, and partly to warn parents about the effects of their careless and thoughtless criticisms of school on their children, I will set down a few cases that have come under my notice.

A boy ten years old fell behind his classes so persistently that the principal of his school, after looking in vain for causes adequate to account for his seeming utter indifference to study, and after exhausting every pedagogical device to interest him in things mundane, sent him to a clinic. There a careful examination was made, and though the boy was found to be but of ordinary mentality, he seemed to possess enough mind to succeed moderately if he would only apply himself. There were no radical physical defects in the way of this, either; no cause appeared but his sublime indifference to study or to any other preparation for life. The reason for this attitude was discovered when he was asked what he was going to be when he grew up and blandly answered, "Nothing; for the world is com-

ing to an end in 1917, and there isn't any use of getting ready to do anything." Then it transpired
that the boy belonged to a family who held a mil-
lennium doctrine that looked confidently for the
near destruction of this world. The boy heard it, believed it, applied it literally to his own case and refused to make any preparation whatever for his
future here. He knew that the sect to which his
parents belonged was misunderstood and criticized,
and hence he kept his doctrines to himself until the
seriousness of his retardation led him to a clinic
where he blurted out his confession. Needless to
say, his parents had had no intention of permitting
their theological doctrines to make such an impression upon their son and took immediate steps to
correct it.

Another case is so utterly ridiculous that only its
cogency as an illustration of how almost unthinkably
trivial causes will affect children's attitude toward
studies, and its actual occurrence in a large city of
the Middle West justifies its restatement. A little
girl, apparently from a very poor and very ignorant
foreign family, did well in all her studies except
geography. Finally, in despair, the teacher sent for
Mary's mother, who duly appeared, an uncultured
ignorant woman, belligerent and not over-refined in
her manner or ideals of life. She heard the teacher's complaint to the end and then almost dazed that
good spinster-lady by remarking with the utmost
complacency that geography was patently utterly fu-

tile, since she herself without it had contrived to consummate a woman's supreme ambition in life by securing a husband, while the teacher, with it, had failed! No wonder that Mary despised geography! It is a compliment to the versatility of the American school-teacher to add that this one quickly recovered herself, led Mary's mother into further conversation, accepted an invitation to visit their home and meet the prize husband, who turned out to be very anxious for his daughter to become a school-teacher because she would earn a large salary. With that as her cue, the teacher led Mary and her father to see the more certain and more immediate value of geography as an asset to teaching, while she pleased the mother by assuring her that it was not an obstacle to the ultimate vocation of matrimony.

Other instances, some more serious and some more ridiculous, illustrating the undesirable effects of home ideals on pupil's progress in school will readily come to mind. The American boy's hopelessness in grammar caused by his father's grandiose assertion that a free-born American did not have to be taught his native tongue; the failure of another in drawing because his commercial parents despised "artists"; the collapse of a girl under a certain teacher because the girl's mother and the teacher crossed swords in some social affair; all these could be developed at length to teach the same lesson of home influences upon the backwardness of some pupils in certain or all of their studies.

Home influences are not limited to inculcation of
ideas. Some of them are physical, definite in their
nature, and serious in their effects. The commonest of these causes are sanitary and nutritional.
What and how a child eats; how many hours, and
under what conditions he sleeps, how much fresh
air he has at his command, any or all of these items
of his daily régime bear heavily on his mental development and often make or mar his educational
course. Being physical, and therefore not always
appreciated as having direct mental bearings, being
distant from the schoolroom, and, therefore, not
easily observable, and being confined to the home,
and hence intensely difficult to amend, such causes
are the hardest of all to deal with effectively. It is
a great help for a teacher in any particular case to
know that home conditions are at the bottom of the
matter. It enables her to put the blame where it
belongs and not to put it where it does not belong.
The following case illustrates how blame may be
misplaced:

Sarah was a girl about nine who came to school
every morning and regularly put her head down on
her arms on her desk and for half an hour refused
to do anything whatsoever. Punishment succeeded
in developing only a spell of stubborn sullenness,
and coaxing was of no avail. If she was left entirely undisturbed, Sarah seemed to fall into a half
stupor from which she aroused herself gradually
and with effort and assumed little by little the duties

of the day. She was always more dull and stupid than the normal children, but behaved well and seemed to try to learn though she suffered from a number of physical defects.

Finally, through the social service department of a clinic, her home was investigated. It consisted of two rooms in a tenement located in the crowded section of a large eastern city. In those two rooms a family of nine persons, father, mother and seven children, ate, slept and lived. How they did it the dwellers in the slums only know. They had no regular bedtime nor meal-times. They went to bed and rose as fancy or the demands of their work dictated. On the table was always a loaf of bread and perhaps some bologna sausage, and on the stove a pot of black coffee or tea. In winter windows were kept closed to save fuel and the conditions of such a sleeping place can only be imagined. From a night in such quarters, Sarah rose, dressed, seized a hasty bite of bread and meat, swallowed some coffee, if there was any, and hurried off to school. There outraged nature asserted itself and the worn-out nervous system racked all night by city noises, disturbances, poisoned air and over-crowded quarters, seized the opportunity in this comparative repose and fell into a kind of stupor.

What this single illustration teaches might be enforced by literally thousands of examples, for thousands of backward children among the six million pedagogically retarded ones, suffer from lack of food, improper food and poor housing. However, the converse, that all poorly fed and poorly housed children are backward, is not true; though in all probability there is a close connection between the two. That coffee-drinking has something to do with low grades in conduct and studies is indicated by Mr. C. K. Taylor's statements concerning four hundred and sixty-four pupils. The general average for conduct for those not drinking coffee was seventy-five and six-tenths per cent., while for all of those drinking it was seventy-three per cent. Those who drank four cups a day averaged only sixty-seven and eight-tenths per cent. In their grades a similar result was found. For the month in which the test was made, the non-coffee-drinkers averaged seventy-three and fourth-tenths per cent., and the drinkers seventy and eight-tenths per cent. Those drinking four cups a day averaged only sixty-three and eight-tenths per cent. Other conditions not conducive to study may have entered into the total situation, but with these figures before us, it hardly seems possible to treat coffee-drinking by children as a matter of indifference. Yet the habit is most common. Doctor Chapin reported that out of two hundred and sixty-two New York school children, ninety-three per cent. had tea or coffee every day, and forty per cent. twice a day. Investigations made in New York, Chicago, Philadelphia, Boston, St. Paul, and other large cities go to show

that about ten per cent. of the school children are
seriously underfed. This comes from several conditions. Some children do not have enough provided at home. Gathered from many sources sta-
tistics indicate that about fifty or sixty per cent.
of city school children do not have enough breakfast, and possibly eight to ten per cent. have no
breakfast. Some of these go home for lunch, but
many either buy penny lunches or do without eating
at noon. In Philadelphia it is estimated that school
children spend one hundred and seventy thousand
dollars annually away from home for lunches. John
Spargo noted that in New York City the girls and
boys bought lunches chiefly composed of pickles,
ice-cream, candy, bananas, bread, bologna and
pickled fish. Some of the boys preferred to gam-
ble with their pennies to spending them for such
lunches, and it is a nice question to determine which
was worse on their morals.

How much such articles of diet affect children's
studies has never been ascertained. That they do
affect them materially for the worse goes without
saying. It seems impossible that brains taking one-
eighth of the blood in the human body could work
well when supplied with an arterial circulation which
must be affected by ferments and toxins generated
from disproportionate amounts of acids and sweets
like ice-cream and chocolates. Education working
on the masses is the only cure in sight for these

conditions. The school-lunch movements not only alleviate present conditions but educate for the future.

A common cause of retardation is the influence of companions. This potent determiner of a pupil's studiousness reveals itself most prominently in college life. When he leaves home for college there to take his life in his own hands, probably to live in a fraternity house where every item of his daily conduct is intimately acted and reacted on by other youths, the overpowering importance of company comes out. Many a college student has been made or marred by his college companions. Many a one has been saved by the simple expedient of changing his lodging or boarding-house and so falling in with a totally new group of men.

This tendency to conform to the ideals of the group, or to the "gang spirit," expressed so prominently in college, is also present in boys of primary-school age. With them home influence usually holds it in check. Sometimes, however, the home fails and the boy suffers in his studies, not because he is naturally bad morally or mentally, but because of untoward or unfair conditions. Any one can feel this truth in the following story:

Allan was a boy born across the water while his father, for business reasons, was in America, where one cause after another kept the father until his boy was ten years old. Allan did not feel the loss of all those ties that go to make fathers dear to their boys and boys dear to their fathers. He had never known them, and besides, his mother and his grandparents made up much that his father could not give. So he grew and played, and went to a private school, and was petted and cared for by all his relatives more than he would have been had his father been at home. He was shielded from all dangers, spent much time with grown people and received and returned a boundless affection for those about him and withal, was as happy as a healthy red-cheeked boy could be.

Then, to him quite suddenly, his mother and he left all the joys he had known so long, and came to America to join the father. The change for Allan can well be imagined. From a country town he came to live in a large city, from fields and woods and rivers, to an apartment house; from a quiet private school, to a hurly-burly American public school.

His father was strange to him and he was strange to his father. His mother tried to make it up to him and managed to do so until the care of Allan's sister took her time. Then came the sorest trial of this little boy's life.

For nearly a year he had done fairly well in his studies, as well as could be expected for a pupil with such a totally new curriculum. Then he began gradually to fall behind his class. All his schoolwork suffered about the same decline. At first the teachers thought it might be temporary, but the lagging continued. The immediate cause of it ap-

peared in his indifference to his studies and his lack
of attention. His teachers noticed that and wondered at it because he had always before been so interested and eager in his strange shy way. Along
with his inattentiveness and backwardness had come
a deep and more subtle change of general attitude.
He was not so shy nor uncertain. He had acquired
a certain self-confidence. He listened to admonitions about study with an air of superiority as if he
had found something better. His parents noticed
the same kind of change and still others with it. He
did not spend his evenings at home, but lived them
on the streets in spite of warnings and finally punishments, neither of which did any good. His deterioration was rapid. In a few months he had
changed from one of the most docile to one of the
most unprofitable boys in school, irregular, tardy,
indifferent, bored; speedily falling into the class of
hopeless retardants. Yet nothing appeared on the
surface to account for this distressing change.

His condition became so bad and the causes so
baffling that he was taken to a clinic for special examination. Nothing was found in his physical or
mental condition that would explain his misconduct or his pedagogical retardation. A social
worker was sent to his home where the above de-
scribed home conditions were found to exist. Then
she went to the school and watched Allan on the
playground. His companions were a revelation.
Instead of associating with neatly dressed boys of

his own social standing, she found he was the hanger-on of a group of ragamuffins most of whom were older than he was, and most of whom were also retarded in their schooling and therefore were still in that school of primary grades. To these boys Allan was a treasure. He brought them cakes, fruit, candies and money he had been browbeaten into taking from home. So pitiably simple-minded was he that he gloried in his membership in the gang and rejoiced in the comradeship of these fellows and his apparent importance in their eyes. To the social worker the whole cruel situation came with the force of a child-world tragedy. The lonesome little foreigner had never played much with boys; they were strange to him and their games stranger still. At school he was an outcast; at home neglected. At the lowest ebb of his spirits when he was ready to make friends with anybody, he fell in with this gang of idlers, who welcomed him as a new source of diversion and exploitation, and speedily impregnated his simple mind with ideals all at variance with obedience, study and honesty. Who could blame this homesick, lonely boy if he accepted the superior wisdom of these older boys and fell a ready victim to their advice and their practises? He felt in every particular like the country boy who plunges for the first time into city life and grows an abnormal sophistication which pities the simplicity of his country home.

Once the cause of Allan's degenerative course was

found out, it was not hard to reverse it. First, his father was given a word or two of advice about paternal duties and the superior efficacy of well-regulated amusements and evenings at home over the too ready resort to the rod. Next, the teacher's help was enlisted and pains were taken to see that the stranger took lessons in American citizenship by learning American games. The effect was immediate and the final effect most satisfactory. Allan regained his normal spirits, returned again to the study of his school-books, and at last accounts was as proud of his new baseball and bat as any young American.

An instance of retardation and moral delinquency of aggravated form is the following. A boy of twelve years, from a most excellent family, of fine physical appearance, and apparently of more than usual intellectual ability, fell steadily behind in his school-work until he was two years behind his class. His father was dead, and on account of certain circumstances, his mother was compelled to give much of her attention to her own father's business. As a result, this boy, Rupert, was left more to his own resources and with less supervision than he would have had with a father and a mother who could give him the usual care bestowed on growing boys. He lived in a beautiful suburb of an eastern city, where the fine physical appointments and the high social positions of the largest part of its residents gave an added sense of security to the parents of sons. But there, as everywhere, the upper classes had their complement of lower classes, and among the latter Rupert found his companions.

How his association with them began is not clearly known. It seemed to date from the visit of a cheap circus to the town. Rupert, like all healthy youngsters, in the nomadic period of his life, was wild about the show, its animals, its performers and its fascinating free life. During the three days it remained, he spent all the time he could down among the tents, was delighted when permitted to carry water for the horses, or to do any other menial task he was asked to do; associated with the circus hangers-on, and met and mingled freely with a class of boys, black and white, whom he had seen before but had instinctively avoided. Their common liking for the circus, its life and its spirit, was a strong bond between Rupert and his new-found friends. He entered into their life with the zest of boyish enthusiasm and the fascination of a novel experience.

After the circus left, the boy continued his close and daily contact with the same gang of boys. Gradually he fell into their ways of doing, and what was not so obvious, but even more serious, into their ways of thinking. He became a part of them, a leader in some respects; fawned upon by them for his superior talents, better clothes and ready supply of money. Inevitably the first pranks degenerated into acts of hoodlumism, and then into petty thieving until the latter practise became quite serious, and included the purloining of large sums from home. Parallel with the moral delinquency went intellectual deterioration and neglect of study until Rupert fell far behind his class. The whole process continued over a period of three years. Punishments were of no avail to compel him to study nor to separate him from his gang. Finally, so serious did his infatuation for his comrades become and so detrimental to his mental life was the effect that he was taken to a clinic for a mental examination.

No physical marks of abnormality, no special mental defects beyond general pedagogical retardation, and no moral deviations beyond those incident to a bad environment appeared. To observe the boy still further, he was placed for a month or more in a special class where no abnormalities developed, and where Rupert showed himself to be amenable to discipline and capable of study. No special pedagogical devices were necessary to secure from him fair work and considerable improvement. The experiment in the new surroundings was considered a sufficient demonstration of the cause of his retardation and he was entered in a very good boarding-school.

There among new surroundings his improvement continued, and at last report he was making good progress, had readily adjusted himself to his new environment and was part and parcel of the new group, entering into the games and ideals of the students as if he never had been afflicted with an almost ruinous and abnormal predilection for a street-gang of low order. His face and his bearing betoken a boy of more than usual nobility in character and breeding. His temporary aberration was due to the power of ideals grafted on his mind by the crowd of boys among whom he inadvertently fell.

The Conversion of a Gang.—These two cases illustrate what can be done by removing boys from the influence of the gang. Sometimes this is not possible and the teacher is squarely faced with the project of converting the gang for the sake of its retarded members. I am not aware that the gang has been very widely studied from this point of view, nor that its value as a pedagogical asset has been thoroughly explored. The following two instances may indicate how the gang may be converted and its members saved to the school, first, by individual efforts, and second, by organized efforts.

In a country town, a group of boys in the upper grades had gradually crystallized into a gang of young vandals, full of mischief, given over to night-prowling and day-loafing, to indolence in school and rebellion against study. Among them it was counted smart to be ignorant and big to neglect openly all school tasks. When any pupil through desire, shame or fear, attempted to get his lessons, he was greeted with sneers and jeers, called "the teacher's pet," and threatened with ostracism from the group. As the town was small and the boys of thirteen to fifteen or sixteen were not many, as the swimming hole, baseball field, woods and streams were common property, it meant much to the one made an outcast by his diligence. The condition was called to the teacher's attention by declining grades and by increasing retardation of certain boys. All the usual methods of stimulation were tried and failed. The situation was becoming daily more serious in the school, had attracted attention outside, and as usual led to a suggestion for a new teacher.

At that point the principal took matters in hand. He began by studying the situation indoors and outdoors. He soon discovered the outlines of the gang and noted that the line of demarcation between the gang and the good students was the same. His first appearance on the playground was made one day at recess when this particular group of destructive imps was bombarding the maple trees with stones from the graveled walks. There was a pause in the throwing, a pretense of picking up more stones to throw, a bravado attempt on the part of the boys to look unconcerned. The principal took in the situation, and in a half querulous tone, remarked, "Why don't you boys set up that old tin pail and see who can hit it at ten paces?" Partly to cover an embarrassing situation the

boys set up the pail and started in to throw per-
functorily. The principal kept the score, the interest warmed up, and by the time recess ended,
the gang was hot in the midst of a contest of throwing, the pail was nearly annihilated, and the principal was one of the gang.

The principal followed up his initiation by spending recesses and noon-hours on the playground. He
introduced, organized and inspired games. He
showed that brains won "prisoners' base," and he
developed generals and generalship as it was never
known in that pastime before. He permitted the
boys and girls to play together and so infused a
spirit of chivalry into the contests. He played ball,
coached the pitchers and showed himself to be an
all-round man. He won their respect and admiration on the playground and, before they knew it,
they found themselves transferring the glow of the
games to the lessons of the schoolroom and there
desiring the same warm approbation from their
principal that he gave so generously to athletic
ability.

It was not long before Saturdays and Sundays
were utilized. The teacher organized hikes, as
they would be called now, taught his boys to camp
and cook, to see curious things in nature, to study
geography in open fields, and history in landmarks.
Gradually the original nucleus expanded until other
boys who formerly did not belong to the gang, were

introduced; and being good scholars, and being found also to be good fellows, they leavened the whole lump with new ideals.

It was not all done in a day nor so smoothly as I have hinted. There were periods of suspense and crises. The great crisis came in a blacksmith shop. It happened that the ringleader of the gang was a big husky son of the town blacksmith, a man of natural force and some influence, but little education. He had rather gloried in his son's leadership against study and listened readily to boys' criticisms of the principal's new tactics, acquiescing in the suspicions and growing sentiment that "A teacher ought to tend to his business and spend his time in study instead of running all over the country with a pack of boys." None of this was lost on the principal who dropped around to the blacksmith shop one day to cultivate the old man. It happened that they were welding steel wagon tires, a heavy laborious job requiring strength, alertness and skill. The temporary helper who swung the sledge was a half useless fellow who was too slow and usually wrong. The smith was in a black sullen humor, and the teacher paused at the door in silence, seeing no propitious opening and not knowing what to do, until the exasperating stupidity of the helper carried him back to his father's blacksmith shop, and his own days at wielding the sledge. Then before he knew what he was doing, when the tire melting hot came off the forge, he sprang forward, seized the great hammer and with a perfect rain of clean-cut blows, the smith and he welded up the neatest joint of the day. The victory over the gang was won right there. What the old man said or did to his boy is not recorded, but thereafter Pete, the leader of the gang, became the teacher's stanchest supporter, though through insufficient brains he could never become a brilliant student.

Organizing the Gang-Spirit for Study.—Of course, we know that every one can not swing a sledge and that a blacksmith shop is not the place for a lady principal, but common sense may glean enough principles from the above procedure to enable a wise teacher to deal with an unruly crowd. The next scene is laid in the city and gives general account of an organized effort to control and direct the gang spirit to study.

Mickey Hogan was short and stocky, older than he looked, red-headed and freckled as his name demanded, and as Hibernian as Irish ancestors and American birth could make him. He was lord of the streets in his neighborhood, a terror to good-doers among his schoolmates, a retarded pupil by choice, not by necessity, and leader of a self-perpetuating gang in the school where he went. The gang had long been the despair of the teachers. That part of the city was little enough conducive to study as it was and retardation was so rife that no artificial stimulation was needed to make it thrive. But the gang did stimulate ideals altogether opposed to intellectual ideals and Mickey was their prophet.

One day an event occurred in his school. He, with some other boys of his age, was called into a room and there met a strange man with scales, measuring-rods, calipers and other curious instruments. Mickey, true to his cult, viewed the proceedings with the superciliousness of a boy inured to the new education, but with trembling in his heart, and a rebellion near to the surface. The man began to put the boys through some measurements and to make comments. His manner was pleasant and businesslike, and since no extra study appeared to be involved in the process which seemed to be concerned with muscles and breathing-power, Mickey got interested in the measurements of biceps and in the tin can for measuring lung-power, that raised up like a gas tank when one blew through the rubber tube. He was eager for his turn and swelled his biceps and squared his shoulders and drew himself up to his full stocky height. When he came to the lung-power machine, he made up his mind to blow it out at the top, but was surprised to find how soon the rising reservoir stopped. Try as he would, he could not muster another breath and the indicator showed he blew less than a boy with a clean face, whom Mickey despised.

"Try again," said the man good-naturedly, and Mickey took a long breath and emptied his lungs into the tube. It was no use. The indicator would stop at about one hundred and seventy-five cubic inches.

Then the man slipped a tape-line around his chest under his arms and measured Mickey's chest expansion. It was suspiciously small. "Too many cigarettes, my boy," said the man in a perfectly matter-of-fact voice, "you're cutting into your wind. You've got a mighty fine build but you won't last at the pace you are going." Mickey was both delighted and frightened. He was proud to be considered "tough," but he did not like to think it interfered with his health and strength. He was sensitive about his short stature and had always taken comfort in his sturdiness. To have it demonstrated by an apparatus that could not lie, and remarked on casually by a man who did not care, placed the judgment beyond dispute.

Mickey listened very attentively to the rest of the man's scheme. It was simple enough. At the end of another six months all the boys were to be measured again. The boy who showed the greatest all-round physical development would have his picture framed and hung up in the schoolhouse hall for all the boys to see and admire. Frequent talks would be given by experts telling the boys how to grow strong. To gain strength meant regular hours, plenty of sleep, plain food, without coffee, tea, much candy, ice-cream or soda-water, and positively no cigarettes or tobacco. It was rather a stiff program for some of the boys and especially Mickey, but he took a big breath and resolved to try it. It was a good thing that he did not then know all the details of the struggle. For the next six months he fought his battles grimly. His eye was single for the physical prize, but his teachers soon noted an improvement in his studies. The reasons for that were many. The chief ones were his improved health, which in boyhood follows rapidly any betterment in hygiene, and the fact that he stayed at home nights to keep out of temptation and having nothing else to do, he studied. What was happening to Mickey was happening in a more or less degree to his followers. All of them were not so determined as he, but they were still following their leader in this new quest for physical might. As a result their attitude changed from indifference to anything good to intense interest in one good thing and to subsidiary interests in many other things. Their studies and conduct improved with the building of their bodies. The talks on hygiene were constantly stimulating. Clubs were organized by university students, and trips were taken to parks and to the outlying country; exercises were given; deep breathing was practised daily; colored button-badges were distributed as marks of honor, and the old gang spirit was captured, tamed and harnessed to works of good instead of evil.

The six months were up at last and Mr. Taylor, the organizer of the movement, now an old friend to the boys, reappeared with his scales, tapes and calipers, and amid many a nervous jest and jibe, the boys went through their tests. Mickey won. He ought to have won. Nobody had been more faithful to the daily exercises than he. He had commanded the admiration of his teachers, too, for his sturdy adherence to study and his advance in school work. Not only had his influence permeated his crowd with new zeal for intellectual things, but he had interested his hard-working father, a man seemingly infinitely removed from school affairs, but who himself had had athletic aspirations in his young days. When Mickey announced that he had won and would have his picture taken, his father was so delighted that forthwith he took his son to a store and bought him a pair of tights with green plush trunks, and in that costume, Mickey, with his arms proudly folded, with his knuckles under his biceps, was photographed and his picture hangs in his school to-day.

CHAPTER VII

THE BACKWARD CHILD IN THE HOME

WHAT star was in the ascendant when Jerrold was born is a question. Surely he was lucky to pass from the blankness of nothingness into a mansion where every tenderness and luxury waited for him. Unlucky he was in the journey, for one leg and one arm were paralyzed. It was bad enough in itself for him to enter life maimed, but his ailment made matters worse. It was astonishing how many hard things in life that helpless arm and leg were able to ward off. Not a task was Jerrold ever permitted to perform for himself. From birth through babyhood nurses and eiderdown were his alternatives. Servants tended him day and night, washed him, fed him, dressed him and kept him helpless all through a pampered childhood, marked not by stages of achievement, but merely by the passage of empty years. When he was seven he was still a baby; when he was fourteen, he was a child of seven. His body grew; he learned to walk by dragging one foot; he could not use one hand; everything that medical science knew had been done for him, but he was a cripple.

At about fourteen, after money had done everything for him except the essential, he drifted into a boarding-school. It is hard to believe that a boy from such a home could be in such a state. At first glance his personal appearance betokened pure imbecility. His face wore the vacuous look of an imbecile; his lips hung ajar, and he drooled saliva like a baby; his clothes were of excellent material but worn slovenly; his left hand was held closed to his side, as useless as the claw of a fiddler-crab; the toe of his left foot dragged on the ground as he walked, or hopped about in his ludicrous efforts to play. To all appearances he was a slouching, helpless, grinning simpleton.

He could not do anything. No royal imbecile was ever more helpless. He had never washed his face and hands, combed his hair, dressed himself, tied a shoe-string or neck-tie, buttoned a button, nor taken a bath unassisted, in all his life. Servants had done it all. They had followed him about, taking his orders, enduring his high temper and childish abuse, waiting on him hand and foot, bringing to him what he required and picking up what he threw down. He ate like a savage, grabbing his food in his hand and thrusting it into his mouth till it was stuffed full, and then champing it like a dog. An extreme case, you say. It was, but a true one in all essentials. His extremity is what makes it valuable, as the end will show.

At school, for the first time in his life, Jerrold fell among boys. They began his training. Since his table manners were so bad, he was given a small table in the corner of a room and a young man ate with him. He was compelled, on pain of missing dessert, to eat with a knife and fork, to chew his food and otherwise to act rationally. Next, he was taught to take a bath under a shower by compulsion, during which the back of a hair-brush wielded by students aided his circulation and sustained his perseverance in the operation. His hands, which were black with grime, were scrubbed with a scrubbing-brush and a repetition of that vigorous method promised unless he kept them reasonably clean. His dressing was taken in hand and he was compelled to put on his clothes and to button buttons. His shoe-strings were laced and tied for him once and then he was shown how he could unhook and hook them without untying or tying them. His teeth and his hair were turned over to his care, and he soon learned to take pride in keeping his hair smooth and his teeth white.

In the meantime his outdoor life was not neglected. He began at the school to play with boys half his age; but he was shamed out of that and introduced to sports more fitting to his years. His fellow-students were patient and good-natured here and he did his best. They undertook to straighten his arm and fingers, invented a brace for his arm, exercised and massaged his fingers into strength and motion, pulled his arm straight and put muscle on it. Jerrold responded nobly to all that. He wanted to be big and strong. He worshiped the big center on the football team and. would obey him with canine docility. In a couple of years he grew by eating, bathing and exercising into a robust boy. His features changed, his mouth closed, his arm gained its powers, his hand its cunning, and he walked, still with the slightest limp, but with his foot flat on the heel and toe.

His studies showed similar improvement. He always had brains but in some respects they had never been developed beyond their baby stage. Travel and association, stories read and told him, had filled his mind with much that was good. His environment had shielded him from evil. His tutors had given him the rudiments. With his adolescent mental awakening had come the greatest increase in his physical powers. The whole exhilaration of the period, natural and artificial, literally and visibly, made of him a new being. Instead of an imbecile, he was a well-dressed, intelligent, cultured young man; still bearing obscure scars and lingering vestiges of his backwardness, but on the whole so nearly normal that he visited a college class composed of teachers and students of abnormal children, entered the room, sat through the lecture, came forward and was introduced to the professor, all before the eyes of the thirty students, none of whom noticed anything unusual in his appearance or conduct.

This case is valuable for illustrating many points. Three of them I want to note especially. First, Jerrold's home was, from the popular point of view, all that could be desired. Not a material comfort was lacking. The boy had everything but training. Second, lacking that, he was unfitted for all higher education. He had not laid the foundations for any kind of study. He had formed no habits of daily routine, and acquired no habits of study. Third, as a consequence, not only his body, but his mind was undeveloped. This should be especially remembered because it is not always clearly understood that mental development begins in the home and comes through such self-help activities as dressing, bathing and eating.

Diagnosis.—Backwardness in a child is often noticed first in the home. With fond fatuity the parents seek to hide the true seriousness of the matter from themselves, or they comfort themselves with the formula, "He will outgrow it." Both policies are wrong. As soon as mental retardation is suspected, a diagnosis ought to be made by a specialist. This insistence admits of no exceptions. No cost in time, trouble and money is too great to obtain it. Any parent who delays for any reason whatsoever is risking the mental life of the child. None but a specialist in mental retardation of children is fitted to make it. When a trustworthy diagnosis is made by a specialist the treatment and training of the child can proceed with the assurance that results will be achieved.

The Home Training.—The training should begin in the cradle. Habits of sleeping, eating and bathing can be developed by an inviolable and implacable order that will lay the foundation for that obedience which is the first essential and always indispensable condition of all training. If there is a time in a child's life when insistence on a mechanical system and a blind obedience is proper it is during infancy, when the child's ·acts are chiefly if not wholly reflexive and instinctive, and consciousness has not reached that acute state where self-will and ideas of justice enter in. Indeed, I am willing to go the length of summing up the aim and method of training the child from birth to his school-age in this: The formation of habits by repetition of self-help activities.

Right habits, then, imbedded in the reflex nervous system of the baby by an unfaltering and undeviating practise of right habits by parents, lay the foundation for all future training. The next part, the ground floor of the character-edifice, is self-help. This again is a fundamental and lifelong lesson. A child must learn to dress himself. I put that first because it is to his interest to dress in order to get out-of-doors. If he has been habituated in babyhood to prompt and expeditious dressing from other hands, he will try to dress himself without delay.

If he is normal, he will succeed with very little teaching; if he is backward, he will require definite instruction with all patience and repeated trials. Remember, too, that such training is also "mental development"; it is "education"; is necessary, fundamental and indispensable to all "higher" acquisition. This truth is revealed by a single glance at the Montessori apparatus with its shoe-strings, buttons and button-holes. Following the dressing, eating can be taken up. A child must eat and it is comparatively easy to bring natural rewards and punishments to bear on him. If he will not eat properly he can be deprived of certain sweetmeats, desserts or luxuries. Because dressing and eating carry with them the motives for their performance I have placed them first in the category of lessons to be learned. Washing the face and hands is not necessary. Often it is a severe trial, especially with boys. Therefore, it is hard to get a child to do it.

Method of Home Training.—I have a feeling that the emphasis on methods of child-training is overdone. It seems to me that in all this self-help, the only method of learning to do is by doing. If a child is to learn to lace his shoes, he must lace his shoes. Let him do it himself and be not over particular how he does it. If he is to put on his trousers who cares which leg goes in first? If he is to dress, whether his waist, or his stockings go first? The whole process has a definite beginning and an end. That is the educational beauty of it.

The hard part is to get the unwilling child to begin, to proceed and to finish. To do that, no new method which will dispense with parental good-humor, patience and firmness, has been, or will likely ever be invented.

The place where method comes in is in the method of proceeding. Generally speaking, all manual lessons should begin with large movements first and gradually proceed to smaller and more detailed ones. Dressing is a suitable exercise except the buttons, shoe-strings, and hair-ribbons. Use of knives and forks is hard for all little people. Washing one's hands and face is not an act difficult to perform and bathing is easy; but face-washing is difficult to teach because boys do not take to it naturally. Because the ideal training can not be found in self-help it must be supplemented with other activities.

The supplementary activities should be play. For the young child under six years of age chores are impossible. He should engage in all forms of outdoor play that involve the large movements of running, jumping, rolling on the grass or ground, climbing, hobby-horse riding, swinging, throwing, playing in sand, and all other games of childhood. The busy mother can not adequately direct the play of her children and she need not worry about it. One thing she must do: Let them play. If they are well, they will play. Even a retarded child will play if he has companions of his own capacity. If no children are available a puppy dog is the next best substitute. Playing with grown people alone generally has a bad effect on children. The gap between their abilities is too great. Emulation disappears and parasitism develops. In general, then, see that the backward child plays with children, toys or animals that *compel him to do his part.*

The Teacher in the Home.—Finally, we come to the teacher in the home. That problem seems easy to dismiss with that solution of all children's problems, that bearer of all their burdens: Mother. But is mother the teacher? Does not a child have two parents and often grandmothers, and older sisters, and sometimes aunts who are schoolteachers? And do not all of these persons lend their conscious and unconscious influence to the training of the child? So important is it that one and only one person should have charge of a child that many of the best child specialists will not attempt to teach any backward child in the home. We can not, then, expect great results from a mother's training if that is interfered with by any others in the home. Still, the mother is the natural trainer and should assume full charge of her child's pre-school education. She may not be the best teacher in the world, but it is better for all concerned if she becomes at least the head-teacher.

A Case of Too Much Teacher.—Mercer was born when his sister was sixteen years of age and thought she knew the same amount about training children that the average young lady of that age thinks she knows plus the amount a girl studying to be a teacher thinks she knows. Therefore, she early took her brother's education in hand. She did not succeed in giving him much book-learning before he was six because his father and mother, both middle-aged, thought he need not be bothered about such matters until he went to school. When he started to school, therefore, the reign of sister Clara, now aged twenty-two, really began. It was a stormy reign. Father and mother kept their hands off the lessons and Mercer found liberty to fight his battles alone. Usually the evening lesson which began so happily in the lamplight of the family circle ended in a domestic storm, with Mercer rebellious, father skeptical, mother resigned and Clara indignant. She said Mercer was stupid and backed her assertion with the testimony of his teachers who said he had learned practically nothing out of books the six months he was in school.

After the evening lesson, Mercer and his father adjourned to the cellar where they had a workshop full of lovely things. At six years Mercer could assemble parts of electric apparatus, arranging cells, wires, coils and bells so they would ring; could attach an incandescent lamp; could start the gas engine and operate it; and could handle tools very well for his age and slight build. His father, who was a machinist, thought he was the smartest boy on earth.

Mercer never played much with other children. He had lived with grown people all his life. That is why the neighbors said he was beyond his years. His mother and sister never let him go outdoors out of their sight. Sometimes, while they sat on the porch, they let him take his little wagon out on the sidewalk and play with other boys. But if a quarrel arose and one of the youngsters slapped him, instead of fighting like a boy, Mercer ran bawling to the sheltering arms of his mother or sister. If he played alone and his automobile wagon upset the same lachrymal demonstration followed. No wonder, then, that the boys called him a baby.

The teachers said he was backward; the neighbors said he was beyond his years; the boys said he was a baby; Binet tests said he was a year above his age; the father said he was smart; the sister said he was stupid; the mother folded her hands, shook her head resignedly and said nothing. The probable truth of the matter was that Mercer was naturally bright, considerably spoiled, retarded in some matters, advanced in others, taught by his father one way, by his sister another, in school another, and on the whole, directed by nobody. He followed his own interests and in the conflict of teachers managed to have his own way. He needed one and only one good teacher and that should have been his mother.

Treatments.—Treatments for backwardness are general or constitutional, and particular or specific. In the first class the treatments affect the whole body and in the second they are applied to particular organs for specific diseases. The latter treatments may be subdivided into surgical and medical. A constitutional treatment aims to build up the whole system by outdoor life, by plenty of fresh air, good food, sleep and play. What these will do in some cases of backwardness caused by neglect or ill treatment almost reaches the marvelous. It will be practically impossible in much of this discussion to keep treatment and training separate; nor is it necessary or desirable to separate them. They merge naturally into cause and effect without effort on the part of the parent. Take this case as an example.

Cyrene was six years old when she was carried to a clinic in the arms of a nurse. She could neither walk nor talk, but crept about the floor and babbled like an infant. She had been picked up in the slums by a charity worker. Her home was a room in a tenement. Her mother had to work daily. Cyrene stayed at home much of the time by herself and was often under the influence of drugs. Neglect, dirt, starvation, accidents, soporific drugs, disease inherited and acquired, had all done their part to stunt the mind of this child almost completely and her body very materially.

She was taken out of her home and placed in a

sanatorium at the seashore for six weeks. There she was given for the first time in her life the care and the nourishment fit for a human being. The treatment she received was not exceptional and peculiar treatment, but just such treatment as any modern institution would give. She was bathed daily, dressed in clean clothes, slept long hours in a bed white and sweet as soap and water, sunshine and sea-air could make it; played all day on a veranda or out in the sea sand; and ate plenty of good, plain, wholesome, well-cooked food. In short she lived the entirely healthful life of a young animal.

In six weeks, what a change! I do not know how many pounds she gained in weight, nor how many inches she grew in height. Neither of those additions was the wonderful part. The change in her mental development without one single conscious effort at special training by her nurses, was the marvel. She learned to walk and to talk, not indeed as well as a normal six-year-old, but wonderfully well for one so recently an infant. She seemed to have grown three years in a few weeks and since that time has continued to improve though not so rapidly.

Cyrene's advance throws into bold relief what is called constitutional treatment. It shows both by their presence and their absence what large and important factors in mental growth are the common daily necessities of life. For her condition, while remarkable because it is unusual, is not therefore an exception to the effect of hygienic living on children in general. Her experience only isolates and therefore presents vividly and clearly the factors of physical and mental growth usually hidden like the pressure of the atmosphere, by their well-nigh universal presence.

Diets for Children.—Backward children do not usually require a diet different from that of other children. However, as many of them suffer from insufficient and improper eating, it seems well to make a few notes on this little understood subject. For convenience, we will treat home-feeding and school-feeding together. Preparing food and eating can be made as highly educational for the mind as beneficial for the body. Buying, cooking, setting the table, eating, washing dishes, cleaning the teeth,—how many and how varied are the lessons grouped about this most ancient, necessary and civilizing process of food-getting! Arithmetic, chemistry, physics, physiology, anatomy, hygiene, ethics, sociology, geography, economics, all these so abstract subjects are directly connected with plain cooking and refined eating; while reading, writing, spelling, grammar, poetry and art may be introduced without much effort. Worship has been connected with all its processes from times immemorial. To get food is the chief struggle of nearly ninety per cent. of all Americans and to secure the dearest food the ideal of nearly all. Out of such an animal struggle and such a sensuous ideal come so much of the greed, the passions and the crimes of our civilization. Food, healthy and healthful, fair-priced and sufficient, well-cooked and well-digested is the solution of many problems within the schoolroom, the home and the great world outside.

Foods, all foods, yield energy. They strengthen muscles and they heat the body. They furnish the fire and steam to the human machine, and do something else no man-made machine ever dreams of doing, namely, they repair the machine itself. Though all yield energy, some foods are especially repairing or tissue-building agents. These are called *proteins* and make up chiefly the white of eggs, the curds of milk, lean meat, parts of wheat, etc. Another group compose the well-known *fat* family, found in fat-meat, butter, olive oil, nuts, corn, wheat, etc. Fat, as everybody knows, is stored in the body for warmth and energy. It does not build tissues like bones and muscles. Another energy-giving food are the *carbohydrates*, like sugar, starch, etc. They are changed into fats in the body. These three, proteins, fats and carbohydrates are the great foods of the body by which it lives, moves and has its being. From the food purchased in the market it selects by its own mysterious processes chiefly these three ingredients and rejects most of the rest. So when the housewife buys a lobster with its shell, its water, its mineral matter, and its protein, fat and carbohydrates, in the last three ingredients the body uses only about one-sixteenth of the whole lobster and about fifteen-sixteenths is thrown away in shell and water. Lobsters are not only dear in first cost, but terribly dear in last cost. When a man pays a dollar and a half a pound for one alive he really pays one dollar and a half an ounce, or twenty-four dollars a pound for the lobster he really gets. Again we see that all food is not food; and to find how much food a child ought to have we must figure on actual, or available food.

To find out how much a girl or boy ought to eat daily we make comparisons with a man doing moderate muscular work which is similar in effect to the play of an ordinary child. The standard of measurement for tissue building is the weight of protein consumed daily, and for energy-giving food the amount of heat the food will develop measured by the *calory*. The calory is the amount of heat required to raise the temperature of one kilogram of water one degree centigrade; or one pound of water four degrees Fahrenheit nearly; or, if the heat should be turned into mechanical power, one calory would raise one ton nearly one and fifty-four hundredths feet.

As a rough average diet for a child we can take the amounts suitable for a child of ten years and vary the diet by increasing the amounts for other children up to fourteen years, but not beyond, and diminishing them for children down to seven years, thus covering those of school age. The average daily ration for a ten-year-old weighing twenty-eight kilograms (about sixty pounds) lies, in round numbers, between three hundred to three hundred fifty grams* of actual or available food after waste is deducted, made up as follows: proteids, sixty grams; carbohydrates, two hundred fifty grams; and fats, forty-five grams; giving altogether about sixteen hundred calories of fuel or heat value. A little later we will show how the calories are calculated from the weight.

For more accurate measurements we may construct a simple table as follows using as a standard the daily rations needed by a man doing moderate muscular work who requires about twenty-four hundredths pounds of protein and about three thousand fifty calories of heat besides.

Person	Per cent.	Protein (Lbs.)	Calories (Carbohydrates and fats)
Man at moderate muscular work	100	0.24	3050
Boy 15 to 16 years	90	0.22	2745
Boy 13 to 14 years } Girl 15 to 16 years	80	0.19	2440
Boy 12 years } Girl 13 to 14 years	70	0.15	2155
Boy 10 to 11 years } Girl 10 to 12 years	60	0.14	1830
Child 6 to 9 years	50	0.12	1525
Child 2 to 5 years	40	0.96	1220
Child under 2 years	30	0.72	915

*One gram, metric system, equals 15.432 grains avoirdupois weight. One kilogram equals 2.2 pounds nearly.

After the question as to how much a child should eat daily comes the question of what he shall eat. First let us show the method of answering that for individuals; then for a typical class. A child of known age should be weighed and measured, two operations easily performed by anybody, and his blood tested by a physician. Then his diet should be arranged to suit his needs. If he is thin, carbo-hydrates and fats should dominate in his rations. If he is fat and flabby, proteins should dominate. The typical dietary given above for a ten-year-old body may be used for an average and deviations from it arranged. For calculating the calories from the weights the following table may be used.

TABLE II

Substance	Calories per gram	Calories per pound
Protein	4	1820
Carbohydrates	4	1820
Fats	9	4040

For classes the procedure is the same for each individual. Then instead of fitting a ration to each child an average dietary is made up for the whole class. To illustrate we will use an actual special class in a summer school. One meal a day was given and, since it was the noonday meal it was calculated to furnish one-half the required daily food. As the weather was warm the menus were fitted to that condition, and ice-cream appears daily, both for its cooling effects and its allurement to pupils inclined to play truant especially from a school held during regular vacation time. Ten menus were arranged and used through twenty-seven days for nineteen children as given below.

Materials for each child for each meal	Proteid (grams)	Fat (grams)	Carbohydrate (grams)	Calories
1. Bread and milk, double portion, ice-cream	31.16	37.00	117.04	769.00
2. Bread, roast beef, milk, ice-cream	32.4	45.38	73.12	774.00
3. Jam sandwich, rice, milk, ice-cream	26.38	36.95	149.29	885.00
4. Hamburg steak, rice, bread and butter, milk, ice-cream	35.16	46.13	118.74	951.00
5. Macaroni and cheese, bread and butter, milk, ice-cream	30.51	65.05	117.31	1019.00
6. Shredded wheat with sugar and milk, bread and butter, prunes and ice-cream	20.85	37.32	147.26	904.00
7. Lettuce sandwich, with dressing, bread and butter, milk and ice-cream	23.17	37.60	105.47	745.00
8. Scrambled eggs and bacon, bread and butter, milk and ice-cream....	31.79	72.72	74.08	866.26
9. Creamed beef, bread and butter, milk and ice-cream	33.64	50.67	78.48	798.00
10. Creamed beef, baked potato, bread and butter, milk and ice-cream	36.33	50.76	100.51	897.00

Total average per portion: proteid, 28; fat, 45; carbohydrate, 115; calories, 881.

It will be noted that the fat is very high, that the average per portion is equal to the total standard daily portion. The fat is mostly derived from milk and butter, which is the most wholesome form for children. The children whose home diet was most lacking in fat were watched carefully and it was seen that they got more butter than the others. Several learned to eat butter for the first time. Again, the values given above took no account of waste. They are based on the assumption that all of the food served was eaten every day which, of course, was not strictly true, a fair amount being lost in changing from platter to plate.

Surgical Treatment for Particular Diseases.— Surgical operations are so clearly procedures of medical men, so technical in character and so remote from the accomplishments of ordinary people that it seems almost a waste of time to consider them here. Yet everybody recognizes instantly what a close connection the parent has with the inception of surgical operations on children. The surgeon can not take the initiative. Patients must be brought to him. Here again, as in medical cases, an early operation may save untold trouble. Adenoids, enlarged tonsils, earache and toothache have such a direct bearing on a child's behavior that the parent often discovers these defects first. If parents understood the same matters much of their prejudice would also disappear. It seems appropriate, therefore, to touch very briefly and popularly on a few of the commoner anatomical ills of backward children where operations may help the permanently backward and very frequently cure the temporarily backward. As adenoids are common we will begin with them.

Though adenoids are absorbed during adolescence, by that time all the mischief has been done and the marks remain for life or must be removed by long and tedious treatment. Therefore removal of adenoids is counseled by nearly all experts. This becomes imperative when the following symptoms appear:

1. Open mouth, especially during sleep, teeth coming crooked, disturbed sleep, irritable humor, lack of attention, nasal voice, flat-chest and constant lassitude.

2. Continual colds, nasal discharge, tendency to sore throats, tonsilitis and bronchitis.

3. Earache and partial deafness or hard-hearing.

4. Nervous symptoms like bed-wetting, stammering, St. Vitus' dance, headaches, night-terrors, etc.

The Teeth.—Dental defects are many and various. Tartar is the commonest, decaying teeth the next, and crooked teeth the next. From one or all of these troubles, according to an estimate based on an investigation of New York City schools, half the pupils in America, or nine million little souls, suffer the agony of horses under the whip pulling with raw shoulders against a collar hard as iron. Happily for both children and horses, humanitarians have already cared for the horses and are diligently considering the children. Many of the later dental evils come from the neglect of the apparently harmless though disfiguring tartar. The true nature of this insidious growth is seen when it is known that tartar is a bacterial growth, a weed-patch in a child's mouth which generally sends with every swallow of food millions of its off-scourings into the child's stomach. In that congenial soil they thrive, multiply rapidly and devour the food intended for the tissues of the child's body. Unwillingly he has become the host of an innumerable company of insolent guests who devour his dainties, leaving him only the scraps at the second table. Tartar, any tartar, is therefore serious and especially the kind that sometimes clings closely around the gums of even the most fastidious tooth-washers, and gradually drives back the gums until the teeth loosen in their sockets. Tartar, too, is a forerunner of decay, another germ disease worse in its malnutritional effect than simple tartar, and infinitely more painful and deterring to any application of the mind. Happily that olden-time, well-known institution, the puffed cheek, the sobbing child, his handkerchief pressed to his aching jaw, the consoling mother and the sympathizing group of playmates, has almost disappeared from child-life like the lost art of patching, or else lingers only in out-of-the-way country places. Or, at least, it ought to be; for no longer in a land of dentists is toothache a visitation of Providence to be subdued with hartshorn or laudanum. Yet it is said that only a few years ago, in a school largely attended by foreign children, some were discovered with many teeth missing, a few with only three teeth left, and one or two with no teeth left.

All decayed teeth should be filled, if possible; or drawn, if the dentist advises it. Likewise impacted teeth due to the second teeth's coming in and pressing upon the roots of the first set, should receive immediate attention as they lead to the most aggravated forms of mischief and sometimes to moral delinquency. Crooked teeth, and indeed the whole jaw, can be straightened. Such work should be done as early as possible after the permanent teeth are cut; for the younger the child the more easily and quickly the jaws change their shape. This form of surgery is bloodless and though irritating and possibly painful, it is infinitely less so than years of the inconvenience, poor mastication, bad articulation and ugliness occasioned by a mouth full of ill-shaped, inhuman-looking teeth only partially hidden by an equally repulsive mouth. Because of such easily corrected deformities what unexplainable acts and habits of behavior must be attributed to the irritation and embarrassment suffered by adolescent boys and girls only an omniscient judgment day will reveal. Certainly, besides probable mental and moral qualities, a good, strong, clean, white, accurately adjusted set of teeth adds much to the physical health, appearance and tone of any person. In this day of dentists and tooth-brushes every child should have good teeth.

Other bad companions come trooping in with adenoids. Of course, enlarged tonsils are common accompaniments. They are located on each side of the throat, and can be seen from the inside when the mouth is open. Located more remotely from enlarged tonsils and adenoids, yet frequently accompanying them, is earache, forming with toothache, the twin-terrors of childish days and nights. The pathological relation between adenoids and earache is visibly seen in the eustachian tube, a small canal running from the throat, through which the germs, already having found a prolific soil in the fevered over-blooded throat, are forced to another spot ideal for colonizing in the middle-ear. Spraying the throat with salt-water or weak germicides and consequent coughing or violently blowing the nose assists the germs in the passage to their safe seclusion in the middle chamber of the ear, where no antiseptic can reach them until they have perforated the drumhead, or tympanum, and a running ear relieves the intense pain of the preceding prosperous growth of the germs known to sufferers as earache. If the earache is recurrent and is permitted to proceed unrestricted or is aided by home-made applications, the hearing may be entirely and permanently destroyed. So serious is it that earache should always have the prompt attention of a specialist.

Arising alike in the home and schoolroom is the problem of home-treatment and professional treatment of physical ailments. At home it expresses itself in, "Shall we send for the doctor?"* and in school, "Shall we send him to the medical inspector?" The answer obviously depends on the nature of the ailment; and the discovery of that on the parent's ability to distinguish simple and unimportant affections from serious ones. How much of this skill can be and should be imparted to laymen may be a question; but assuredly those who are charged with the welfare of little people ought at least to know the characteristic symptoms of common contagious diseases.

Colds, for example, are either simple ailments or the forerunners of serious diseases. If a cold is accompanied with continually weeping eyes, a persistent avoidance of light, it likely presages measles; if accompanied with extremely high fever, hard dry cough and soreness all over the body, it means grippe; if a sudden discharge in thick bloody shreds appears from the nose, dread diphtheria is indicated. If the cold is accompanied by a paroxysmal cough rising to a whoop, the signal is almost certain for whooping-cough. Colds and coughs also accompany adenoids. In general any persistent cold, or habitual colds and coughs are danger-signals and should call for investigation and treatment.

* For a simple treatment of this whole subject see *When to Send for the Doctor*, Lippert & Holmes, Lippincott Company, Philadelphia, Pa.

Sore throats are common and may mean much or little. A highly inflamed throat with patches is not necessarily dangerous. If vomiting comes on with high fever, scarlet fever is signalized. Swollen glands in the neck behind the jaw and a gray white "film" inside the throat mean diphtheria. If the tonsils are swollen and studded over with numerous yellow spots tonsilitis is coming on. If the tonsils are very red and large, so large it is difficult to open the mouth, quinsy must be suspected.

Headaches are always serious because they interfere with a child's study and because they are symptoms of other perhaps dangerous conditions in the child's body or his environment. Any teacher can discover these causes by observation, questioning, and experimenting with foods, ventilation, light, play and naps in school.

Investigations in one school system showed that children with skin diseases were more often backward than those with poor eyesight. Hence, the discovery and treatment of skin affections impinges closely on scholastic duties. One hundred years ago all skin diseases were supposed to come from "bad blood." Now we know that many are due to germs securing entrance through the pores of the skin. If skin eruptions come in the form of small red pimples tending to run together, growing moist and itching intensely, eczema is the disease. If the irritation is confined to the head, suspect head lice. If it comes between the fingers or toes, and if a brown-black, zigzag line from an eighth to a half inch long appears, send the child away immediately before it communicates the itch to others. Ringworm, another contagious skin trouble, is early known by the circular direction of the eruption. Scaling of the skin may mean simple dandruff, if from the hair, or eczema, or the result of measles, or of scarlet fever. The last is especially dangerous. Chicken-pox usually comes on without much warning. The small, rose-colored pimples turn to blisters in four hours' time, so the disease, a very contagious one, develops often under the teacher's eyes. Pinkeye is hardly a skin disease, but reddens and swells the eyelids and colors the eyeball a pinkish red. It runs through a school like wildfire, and like all the other contagious diseases, should be detected as early as possible and the sufferers sent immediately to the school doctor. These most common diseases will serve to illustrate the need and kind of knowledge teachers and parents should have to protect their children from contagion and useless suffering.

Beyond these suggestive treatments it does not seem necessary to go. The treatment of earache and adjustment of eye-glasses are so common and the procedure so well known that they do not require special consideration. From this discussion it is hoped that the teacher and parent will derive the general principle that commands all persons concerned with children *never* to attribute their backwardness or badness to *wilfulness,* but always in the most persistent, aggravated and aggravating cases, to believe in and to search unremittingly for some physical defect in the child or outside of him. If that, when found, is removable, the child can be cured. If not, he can not be cured. In either case it is not his fault. And here, for the sake of millions of misunderstood children I must yield to the temptation and set down this universal negative: *No child is ever a bad or a backward child through his own fault.*

CHAPTER VIII

THE CLINICAL DIAGNOSIS OF BACKWARD CHILDREN

IN all the previous chapters of this book we have proceeded inductively in the study of backward children. We have brought forward concrete cases to illustrate types and to show how these children were diagnosed and treated. The cases are taken from the common experience of the schoolroom and the home and were chosen because of their striking features which would command attention, and which would set forth underlying principles and in such relief that they could be grasped and applied to other similar but milder cases of the same types. Statistical studies, tables, means and averages, on which all true and exhaustive scientific studies of such matters must ultimately rest, might have been given. For parents and teachers, however, the ultimate is not a statistical table, but the real individual; not an average, but a human being to be saved; not a method applying on the whole, but a definite process to be used once, and only once, to be rejected if it fails, and discarded when it succeeds. Of necessity, such a treatment of the subject did not permit the erection of a close and

162

carefully articulated system of etiology, diagnosis, classification, treatment and training. It is there in germ, but is merely suggested and appears through the illustrations. We will now turn to a more detailed description of the clinical diagnosis.

The Process as a Whole.—The process of diagnosing backward children begins with casual, crude and rough approximations made by unskilled observers, and moves on toward systematic, precise, scientific measurements made by experts. No one should be confused by the fact that several organizations and many subordinate processes are described. At bottom, from the casual opinion of neighbors to the seasoned judgment of an expert, all of them rest on the problem of the child's social fitness or unfitness. Can he ever support himself by his own efforts in society at large? is the fundamental question. It is involved in the definition of feeble-mindedness, and for the teacher and for others responsible for the unfortunate, it is the question paramount. If by any means he can be made self-supporting, though he may never read or write, then he has the same right to schooling as any other child who is fitted in public school for citizenship. If he never can become self-supporting in society at large, then all his years of public school learning are futile, a waste and worse than a waste, robbing him of his opportunities to develop his manual and industrial faculties for life in an institution and stealing time from normal children who will become self-supporting. Social fitness is the one requisite; and in judging this qualification the observations and opinions of common people and especially the tacit attitude of the child's peers on the playground, have more weight than would at first appear to one who thinks this matter wholly an academic and technical one.

This can also be seen from the definition of feeble-mindedness. The Royal College of Physicians of London define it as "a state of mental defect from birth, or from an early age, due to incomplete cerebral development, in consequence of which the person affected is unable to perform his duties as a member of society in the position of life to which he is born." It will be noted that there is a mental defect and that it is incurable, and that it is marked enough to prevent the sufferer from making his living in ordinary society. These two items mark the essentials of amentia, or feeble-mindedness.

Let us now take a bird's-eye view of our whole problem. Here he is before us—a backward boy. That much we know by the judgment of parents, neighbors, friends and school grading. Let us say he is ten years old and in the second grade. What is our task? First, we must diagnose our case. Second, we must apply the proper treatment. That is, to put the matter in pedagogical terms, we must find out what kind of backward boy we have and then we must develop him to his fullest capacity. More specifically we must first and fundamentally determine whether he is temporarily backward and will under right training catch up with his fellows in the race of life, or whether he is permanently backward and can grow only so far in his mental capacity and then will stop.

What We Measure in Classifying Backward Children.—Those two words "mental capacity" need a little more consideration. They bring up the problem of just what we are trying to determine. Is it the child's *present* intellectual attainments, his knowledge of reading, writing and arithmetic? Not primarily. Sometimes he is too young to do any of these and yet is backward. Anyhow the school examinations would settle that. Is it his *present* mental capacity—his *ability* to learn reading, writing and arithmetic? Binet says it is, but immediately recognizes the fact that such a quality is changeable from year to year and hence can not in itself give a final basis for calling any child permanently retarded. Neither can it furnish a basis for a prolonged course of training. No, the quality we are seeking to measure in this ten-year-old boy is neither present intellectual attainments in themselves and by themselves; nor present mental capacities in themselves and by themselves. It is something far more difficult and subtle, requiring not only skill and fine judgment in the examiner, but also the gift of prophecy based on long and wide experience. We are seeking something analogous to the latent forces residing in an acorn. We are trying to analyze the acorn, to determine its powers, real and potential, and to predict, if it is placed in a suitable soil in a salubrious climate, what kind of oak it will be when full-grown. That is what we are trying to determine in our ten-year-old backward boy; not alone *how* backward he is, not alone his reading, writing and mathematics, not alone his present physical and mental powers but his present potentialities.

Not "What is he now?" but "What will he be at puberty when all his mental faculties have reached their maturity?" is the primal and unwavering question we must keep before our minds. All we do and all we ask must unfalteringly be directed toward that one moment. Nor should any favorable or unfavorable item swerve our judgment unduly from its goal. The degree of backwardness, for example, must not betray us into a hasty judgment. Here on the table is a baby, unable to walk or talk, cooing excitably over some blocks, so young psychically that she is not free from the baby grasping-reflex and will close her hand involuntarily over my fingers placed in her palms. Though she screams to seize the blocks before her eyes she can not overcome the instinct to close her fingers and so holds on tightly and keeps on screaming. She is psychically less than a year old; yet she is past her sixth birthday. Is she permanently retarded? Specialists hesitated to say so and hesitated a year after she was under their close observation. In six weeks she learned to walk and to talk and her progress has remained rapid. What will she be at thirteen or fourteen? Such a case is exceptional and I cite it to bring out the point. On the other hand, here is a low-grade idiot ten years old. The prognosis or prophecy is easy. Still another boy is fifteen, past puberty, and his attainments under the best conditions are those of a middle-grade imbecile. Again the diagnosis is easy. No prediction is involved. He is now what he always will be. His potentialities have all become actualized. He is a middle-grade imbecile.

The Oral Examination.—The services of a technically trained expert are not required to make the preliminary survey or oral examination of the case. It consists of a series of observations, and a series of questions and answers. The questions should seek to uncover the causes of backwardness first, by covering the child's pedagogical history; secondly, his life history, giving an account of his present social capacities like play and work; of his individual capacities like self-help; of his moral character; of his diseases, past and present; and of his infancy and of his birth-conditions. This leads naturally to the third item, his family history dwelling on the mental and nervous diseases of his parents, grandparents, uncles, aunts, brothers, sisters and cousins. The last item is always important and sometimes decisive in its testimony as to the temporariness or permanency of the back-

wardness under discussion. How much feeble-mindedness is caused by birth conditions and by circumstances in life, is a question of grave doubt. All
writers admit that the proportion is small.

Heredity.—When we turn to heredity proper
much of the doubtfulness affecting the other two
stages of causes vanishes. The supreme fact that
permanent backwardness is chiefly due to mental
defects of parents seems to be established beyond
doubt and continual researches tend to raise the per-
centages of cases caused by them. The per-
centages vary from about sixty-six and two-thirds
per cent. to one hundred per cent. That is, some
authors suggest that two-thirds at least of all
the feeble-mindedness in the world could be eliminated in a few generations by proper public
sentiment and sufficient legislation adequately enforced to prevent the propagation of the mentally
unfit. Some few insist that nearly all of it would
disappear. Out of thirty-five medical men examined in England by the Royal Commission of
1904, twenty-five asserted their belief that feeble-
mindedness was almost, if not wholly a hereditary
disease. The other ten who placed environment before heredity as a casual factor had had very much
less opportunity to study the facts. Modern biological theories tend more and more to confirm the
opinion of the twenty-five experts. A few scientists
insist that feeble-minded people are a distinct variety
of the human species, and if they were left to them-

selves to propagate their kind, would develop a separate race of imbeciles. All of this evidence tends strongly to the belief that amentia is wholly hereditary and that no diseases, wounds or accidents happening to the individual in his lifetime, at birth, or later, can make an imbecile out of a child with a normal brain. This, however, is a disputed point which may be ultimately insolvable. For, granting that certain diseases like cerebral meningitis will inevitably leave a mark upon the mind of the afflicted child as ineradicable as the scar tissue on the cortex, still it can be plausibly argued that this germ disease would never have arisen had not the brain been natively weak and, therefore, susceptible to the attacks of the disease. Much support is given to this theory by the fact that the sequelæ, or evil results, of scarlet fever and other illnesses, may leave the special nervous end-organs like eyes and ears permanently affected and yet not be able to mar the strong central brain. Examples of such cases will readily occur to all. Laura Bridgman, and later Helen Keller, are brilliant ones. Malnutrition and marasmus may be urged as causes of feeble-mindedness arising after birth. Here again the same kind of counter-argument can be used and supported to some extent with some degree of force by the general assertion that the healthy brain always demands its toll of sustenance even at the expense of all other organs in the human body; that when men die of starvation all their organs except the

brain perish from want. The brain, like the mon-
arch of a kingdom, demands its tax from all the
rest. It starves last.

The Physical Examination.—After the inquiry
into the personal and family history comes the physical examination. While it must be made in part at
least by a regular physician, it need not be a medical
diagnosis. It is safest merely to note symptoms
or suspicions of symptoms to be fully studied later
by a specialist. The examination consists, first, of
a full description of the personal appearance of the
child; secondly, his principal measurements; thirdly,
his chest-expansion, grip of his hands, and his power
to resist fatigue; fourthly, the acuteness of his special senses, especially sight and hearing. This
makes up the first part of the examination which
any clinicist can give. The second part is the medical examination, and should be performed by a
regularly licensed physician. It includes tests of the
heart, lungs, throat and nose, stomach, intestines,
liver, kidneys, genito-urinary organs, and a search
for any constitutional or nervous diseases. The
purpose of this whole examination is twofold; it is
made to discover two classes of physical defects.
The first are removable and hence are associated
with and are signs of temporary retardation. The
second are inborn, are not removable and are signs
of permanent retardation.

Can the teacher learn by the physical marks alone
to distinguish temporary backwardness from per-

manent backwardness? In some low grades of imbecility and in all grades of idiocy, yes. In the
grades of moronity, or light feeble-mindedness, no.
The marks on the bodies of these high-grade classes
are no more numerous nor prominent than with normal persons. Recently a daily paper presented the
picture of an apparent imbecile. There was the
open mouth, front teeth very wide apart indicating
the absence of other teeth, the thick low-growing
hair hiding the upper part of the ears, attached ear-
lobes, drooping eyelids, and the vacuous look of the
vacant mind. Further reading discovered the fact
that it was really a photograph of a young society
woman belonging to one of the best families. This
caution is thrown against the too ready and too easy
judgment of a child by his external appearance. Bad
manners, dirty face and hands, unkempt hair, common ugliness are none of them at all significant of
imbecility, nor of the opposite virtues of mentality.
In cases of true feeble-mindedness the uglier the
child is, the more hope is there of educating him; the
comelier he is, the less the hope of making much
progress in his training.

The Physical Marks of the Typical Imbecile.—
The typical feeble-minded person carries about in
his body marks that, to the practical eye, immediately catalogue him with unerring certainty. These
marks vary in number and prominence from grade
to grade of mentality. The idiot presents them with
pitiable obviousness; the imbecile in a lesser degree;

and the moron only obscurely. Probably no one individual ever possesses all the physical defects of feeble-mindedness. To describe them, therefore, we must imagine a typical case of middle-grade imbecility and making that the standard, expect in general that those below him will possess many of the defects in a more marked degree, and those above him in a less marked degree. Further, we must warn the student that probably not one of the defects to be named are *peculiar* to mental defectives, but that each one of them might be duplicated somewhere in the world in some normally-minded person. One swallow does not make a summer but it requires multitudes of the season's signs to mark the change from spring. So one physical defect does not make a person feeble-minded; but a whole mass of irremovable physical defects found in a *backward* child marks feeble-mindedness with almost fatal certainty. Hence, the caution must go out against, first, judging by physical marks without *backwardness;* secondly, against judging by one or a few marks and not by a systematic examination of the whole body; and thirdly, in the lesser stages of retardation, against basing the final decision for permanent backwardness on physical marks even with a history of backwardness included. With these limitations, the ordinary teacher or parent can do at least two things; first, can be instantly directed to the study and further examination of a backward child and so save it from false treatment and detrimental training, and secondly, confirm to a large degree a suspicion of feeble-mindedness by merely looking closely at a child.

General Appearance.—Even to the most casual and most unskilled observer there is something decidedly abnormal in the general appearance of a typical imbecile. If the observer were asked to point out just what it is that marks out this poor soul from normal people, he would probably be at a loss to do it without systematic practise in the art. That comes from the little-noted fact that people look at each other only very generally and describe individuals only in comparative terms. "Tall," "short," "heavy," "light," "dark hair," "large head," *really mean nothing* as descriptions of persons. I have frequently placed a child before a class of teachers, have asked them to look at the child for fifteen minutes and then tell me what the child was like. The variety of answers received was bewildering. Fat and thin, light and dark, tall and short, large for his age, small for his age, and many other equally contradictory judgments can be derived from persons who observe daily all sorts of children. Such experiences suggest that observing children accurately is an art to be diligently acquired, that wherever possible measurements be made, and that terms as accurate as possible be used, amplified with phrases; for example, not "tall," but "tall for a child of nine," if a measurement is not given, with the implication that the average height of a nine-year-old is the one given in some standard chart like Hastings'.

With these cautions we are ready to take another look at our typical imbecile to discern what it is in his personal appearance that impresses us. To do that we will proceed with a systematic survey, measuring first his height and weight, then looking at his skin, then his posture, then his gait. After that we will proceed to details of hair, skull, eyes, ears, nose, mouth, teeth, tongue, hands and feet. By that time we ought to know something of his characteristic marks.

His Complexion.—In the first place, probably the most striking quality about his general appearance is his peculiar opaque, ashy complexion, due to his poor circulation and his harsh, thick-looking skin which is easily broken, giving ready rise to infection and furnishing a congenial soil for parasites, and giving off, in some cases, a peculiar odor, which is so pronounced that an expert can diagnose imbecility by simply entering the room where such a child has been for a little time. Excellent diet, free exercise and frequent baths will to a large extent overcome all these defects.

Along with the skin the posture makes its impression on the eye. The head is usually inclined forward and to one side, the shoulders droop forward, the hands swing listlessly at the sides, the knees are bent and the whole attitude reminds one of the ape. Walking does not improve matters. The feet drag listlessly, the toes scrape on the floor, the arms swing pendulum-like, and the whole movement proceeds aimlessly and without certain decision as to point of destination or the path of reaching it. The imbecile is clumsy in all movements, slow in running, falls frequently, and shows in every act the one great characteristic of flabbiness in all his thinking and doing.

Various Bodily Organs.—The various organs furnish their detail of defects to fill in the picture. Beginning at the top, we find skulls are too large or too small; too short and too long; the first because of water usually in the cavities of the brain; the second, not because of any pressure on the brain, but because the brain will not grow; the third often from malnutrition in babyhood, giving the box-shaped skull; and the fourth from malformation of brain. The technical names for the four types are microcephalic, hydrocephalic, brachycephalic and dolichocephalic. Though popularly these shapes of skull are thought to be highly important as betrayers of mental defects, they are in fact quite indecisive and in themselves form no criteria of brain defects at all. If the brains are there and in working order it matters little how they are shaped. Napoleon, it is asserted by some, was slightly hydrocephalic. A professor in one of our colleges is markedly dolichocephalic and is very able. Great musicians are said to be usually brachycephalic. Only when other abnormalities of character and conduct appear are these departures from the usual significant. In this connection it might be remarked that the hair is either very sparse or very thick, fine and silky or coarse and wiry, and that the color is not significant.

The Special Sense Organs.—The various organs of special sense come next. The eyes may be small and set near together, or far apart, often defective and sometimes one is one color and the other another color. The ears are thought to be very significant. The lobes are frequently attached or grown to the cheek; the shell is badly formed with little hard knots of cartilage at the top called Darwinian tubercles, because they are thought to come from ape-ancestry; the whole ear may be excessively large or excessively small, may stand out from the head, and may be misplaced, too far back or too high up on the side of the head, though the shape of the skull will often give this effect if it is low or flat at the back. The nose is usually flat at the bridge and wide in the nostrils, though again the opposite may be true and the nose present a keen appearance with thin nostrils. I have never seen a feeble-minded child with a Roman nose, even among Jews, though of course there may be some. The mouth is large and coarse with thick lips, or strikingly small with knife-blade lips. The marked symptom is slavering with sores at the corners of the mouth and cracks at other parts of the lips. The teeth are crooked, peg-shaped, decayed, some absent from babyhood, and sometimes too many present, even to the extent of forming a double row on each jaw. The tongue is thick or thin and pointed, and cut with deep fissures.

The hands are the peculiar organs of human intelligence and as such furnish the surest indicator of the deficient mentality of the imbecile. His hands are typically weak, flaccid, useless, listless, lying about as if they did not belong to him; if well kept, with smooth tender skin, and ladylike fingers, feeble of prehension and likely not to oppose themselves to the thumb in any decided fashion at any time, and not at all for years after birth. The corresponding fingers on the two hands may be of different shape, are sometimes deformed, webbed and lacking; the ends are clubbed and the nails brittle. More significant than their appearance is the imbecile's attitude toward his hands. Normal people find them useful; to him they seem to be insignificant appendages as useless as those of a medieval court-lady and as devoid of purpose as the tail of an elephant. And all of this has come about because they have not been energized into countless activities by a normal and active brain behind them to tasks that have curved the fingers and thumbs like a sailor's ready to grasp a rope. Even after mere imitative training has taught the muscles certain manual habits, there still remains a lack of that decisive prehension so naturally the property of normal minds. Descending to feet we have little to add except to note that flat feet are common, that a broken-down instep seems to indicate a broken-down mind, and

to repeat that the flabbiness of the hand and all other
muscles extends itself to the cold, bloodless pedal extremities, making them peculiarly liable to frost-
bite.

Mental Tests.—The third examination is the
mental test proper. Not that eye-examinations and
head-measurements are not mental tests, but here we
come to tests that have always been associated with
the mind as measures of intelligence. They may be
divided into three kinds; first, pedagogical tests;
second, non-pedagogical tests; third, tests for specific defects in particular mental processes; and, unless such tests have been included in the physical
examination, tests of the special senses. The pedagogical tests are just the ordinary schoolroom examination questions—reading, writing, grammar
and arithmetic. The fact is that the pedagogical
tests are just as good as many others specially elaborated for measuring general backwardness. If
for example, a ten-year-old boy has been exposed
continuously to four years of schooling and can do
only second grade work and no special cause accounts for his deficiency, he can be safely counted
on to be two years retarded in his general mental
growth. Neither, in all probability, will any special
talent in some particular direction vitiate this judgment nor disappoint the expectation that he will
show the same degree of retardation by other systems of tests. In short, school grading, applied to

a large number of children under the same conditions, measures their mental capacities and predicts their future adjustments to society with fair accuracy.

Other tests have been formulated to measure the mental capacities of children independent of their school learning. How far they succeed is a question. The system best known in this country was formulated by two Frenchmen, Monsieur Binet and Monsieur Simon. The final form of the tests consists of five questions and tasks for each normal child from three years old up to fifteen, or mental maturity. An elaborate system of grading defines the child's mental stature. If he is two years or more behind his fellows of the same age, it is assumed that he will never make up the lost ground, and so is mentally defective. These tests are simple, compact, easy to apply and measure mentality in terms of normal children's ages. For these and other accidental reasons Binet's tests have spread far and wide. One stricture on their application can be made with a fair degree of safety. They should not alone decide the feeble-mindedness of any child. Binet himself did not intend them for such a purpose and specifically warns against such a contingency. Taken in connection with physical conditions, environmental influences and heredity, they are probably quite as accurate as pedagogical tests and are more convenient to apply.

Signs of Permanent Backwardness.—Though we now come to what might be supposed to be signs of mental deficiency most easy to discover, namely, the mental signs of permanent backwardness, as a matter of fact, we have reached the most obscure and most difficult portion of diagnosis. For this kind of mental deficiency does not show itself in some peculiar and limited mental defect perfectly obvious to the examiner. As the definition indicates, feeble-mindedness is such a pervasive, such an all-inclusive disease that it can not be diagnosed from one class of symptoms or signs. Here again we meet the same quality which is manifested especially in the higher grades of mental deficiency. I have now in mind a girl fourteen years old, well-formed in every respect, beautiful of face, sweet and mild-tempered, expressing in her repose and poise a mind and character above her years, with no mental defect whatever showing in her exterior appearance, or in her manual work. Yet this girl, who in all manual work shows no want of any ordinary mental powers, soon displays by her talk, by almost infinitesimal traits of manner and silliness of smile, that "something is wrong." What is it? It is an evanescent something, a general tone, a continuous permeation of everything she does with a "lack." "She has a lack" is the paradoxical truth about the matter, though what that lack is, is hard to put down on paper because it does not appear in any of her physical attributes but lies hidden somewhere

in her mind and character and colors her whole active life.

General Signs of Permanent Backwardness.
—Probably the best way to come at the peculiarities of the feeble mentality is to point out the
first and greatest defect. It is *slowness*. But here
again we are in danger of saying at once too little
and too much; too much because many normal people are slow in their thinking processes yet have the
capability not only of maintaining themselves in society but of advancing very materially through years
of persistent toil. The mental defective lacks the
persistency. He is slow and flighty. We are in
danger of saying too little because the slowness is
not always in the mental processes themselves but in
their development. The mental defective will sometimes reply quickly enough; indeed he will exhibit
a certain smartness and wit in his answers or observations, especially if the questions fall within his
limited capacities and if he is of the excitable
and susceptible type. In fact, it is easy to de-
ceive a whole room full of careful observers by
putting questions to a feeble-minded child in their
presence, each question lying within the powers of
the child and worded in such a way that he gets a
hint of the answer, though all the questions may be
new to him in the form in which they are asked.
The slowness lies not always in the working of mental processes like perceiving, remembering, imagin-
ing and reasoning when these powers are present

and items of knowledge are not being learned, but in the development of these processes in the life of the child. Therefore, the mental growth of a permanently retarded person has been likened to that of the normal child except that the growth does not *proceed so rapidly and does not proceed so far.* Hence, we find that Binet defines mental retardation of this kind in terms of normal minds of younger age. To put it the other way round, every normal child is born deaf, dumb, blind and an idiot except that it has in it potentialities which will develop under proper environment to what nobody on earth can predict. Set up all the babies of the world in a row and who can tell which will be the leaders of the world forty or fifty years hence? On the other hand, the mental defective is born deaf, dumb, blind and an idiot, and either remains an idiot, or slowly grows into an imbecile, or else a moron, reaching those upper limits in twelve or fifteen years and halting there for all the rest of his life. Within certain fairly well-defined limits his future can be prophesied and this prophecy we have called the diagnosis. His progress over this limited way is fairly well divided into stages by his years and these likewise have been marked out and described more or less accurately, though work of this kind is still going on and details of his picture are being filled in each year. The signs of his mentality are given in the following composite table made up from a number of authors:

*A Bird's-Eye View of Grades of Feeble-Minded Chil-
dren Correlated With the Ages of Normal
Children*

I. MORONS.

    1. High-Grade Moron.—Educable in elemen-
tary school work; can write simple letters;
can be trained in manual and intellectual
arts; can not plan for the future. Equals
normal child of twelve years, or eleven
years.

    2. Middle-Grade Moron.—Can be trained in
the manual arts; is two years or more retarded in school work of the simplest
kind. Equals normal child of ten years,
or nine years.

    3. Low-Grade Moron.—Can be trained in in-
dustrial and simplest manual occupations;
can do errands and light work; can not
learn to read or write except the simplest
words. Equals normal child of eight
years.

II. IMBECILES.

    1. High-Grade Imbeciles.—Can do tasks of
short duration; wash, scrub, sweep, etc.,
but nothing higher. Equals normal child
of seven years.

    2. Middle-Grade Imbecile.—Improvable in self-
help and help to others, that is, can be
taught to wash himself, eat, etc.; can do
only the simplest tasks; can guard himself
against common dangers. Equals normal
child of six years, or five years.

    3. Low-Grade Imbecile.—Plays a little, but can
do nothing else without supervision.
Equals normal child of four years, or
three years.

III. IDIOTS.

    1. High-Grade Idiot.—Eats with discrimina-
tion, rejecting what is not food; can not

protect himself against common dangers.
Equals normal child of two years.
2. Middle-Grade Idiot.—Able to feed himself,
but will eat almost anything. Equals normal child of one year.
3. Low-Grade Idiot.—Not able to walk, talk or
move; will swallow whatever is put into
his mouth.

Some Particular Marks of Backwardness.—To
the description of these general capacities we may
add a few words concerning definite processes of
the mind. For it often happens, especially with a
certain class of imbeciles called *idiotes savants,* or
learned idiots, that they possess wonderful powers
in certain directions. So the ordinary defective may
possess ordinary capacities in several directions but
be entirely or largely wanting in other directions.

Usually his perception is present but dull, dropping down to greater and greater dulness as we fall
to lower grades of mental incapacity. Training is
necessary to get the defective to see and hear sights
and sounds which the ordinary child perceives instantly and reflexly. His memory is almost always
pronounced "good" by his relatives and friends.
They mean by that that he remembers small items of
experience which, on account of their unimportance,
are speedily swallowed up in the larger issues of life
as it is lived by normal people. Another talent as
frequently noted by friends, is the feeble-minded
child's aptitude for music. As rhythm permeates all
life, so also does it flow through all grades of mental
deficiency, reaching in the morons sometimes to

splendid abilities in classical music, and in a few cases, to a positive genius in rendition. Music is a most valuable means of training mental defectives and the band of a feeble-minded institution is always one of its happiest features. Yet the players can not compose, for their constructive imagination is lame, halting, and usually busied when it acts at all with fantastic and childish schemes, or with vain-glorious dreams of self-aggrandizement, though sometimes those talented in manual work will plan material things, and moral imbeciles will scheme diligently how to do some mischief. If such activities can be called reasoning, mental defectives have reason, but it amounts to no more than mere cunning and to practical wisdom capable of seeing the means to material ends but failing in the higher realms of abstract thinking, and never able to look forward through the years and conserve present good for future needs of self or others. On the whole, through all stages of mentality from idiots up, these capacities vary as they vary in growing normal children, and we can always best measure the power and responsibilities of these little folk, no matter how old they grow, by assigning them to their proper psychological ages and then asking, "What would a normal boy or girl do at the corresponding age?" For instance, if it is a middle-grade imbecile boy we are considering, we must ask, "What would a seven-year-old normal boy do, or be?"

Besides defects in the intellectual processes of

these children, defects in feelings, instincts and emotions often appear especially in the lower grades. The idiot lacks from the beginning the simplest life-preserving instincts; he must be taught to eat, and the lowest grade will eat anything put into his mouth. The higher grades often lack the social instincts. All of them are nearly always egotistic, living in a little world bounded by those interests that closely attach themselves to self and its immediate satisfactions. Vanity, egotism, love of notice and of notoriety are their petty vices, often leading them into ludicrous acts, and occasionally into acts of unpremeditated but desperate violence. One low-grade imbecile always follows visitors through his department of the institution where he is kept, solemnly imitating the official guide in all his acts and gestures. Another tried to bribe an officer at an exhibit to mark his piece of work with a card crediting him with mentality a grade higher than he really was. He did not dream of asking to be made normal. Another set fire to some buildings merely for excitement and the possible chance to play the hero. All of these instances are revelations of the instinctive stages in which these queer people live, as well as instances of failures of that volitional power which would keep similar impulses in normal people safely hidden from the light of day.

Indeed, the final mark of feeble-mindedness lies more in the will than anywhere else. In the last analysis it is a matter of character. Almost every

mental aberration, and every foolish feeling of the
feeble-minded might be duplicated in the myriad of
feelings and foolish thoughts of normal people who
nevertheless have the power to suppress them
always to some degree, and usually to a degree
consonant with their living and moving in ordinary
society. Everybody is in some degree and on some
occasions feeble-minded. Fatigue reduces the best
minds to that state; a terrible event, stage fright,
sudden awakening, extreme embarrassment, reduce
some people to a state of mind very similar to the
almost constant inner experience of the feeble-
minded person whose field of attention is limited always and whose mind stops dead under any, for him,
undue pressure. But the normal person is not *too*
feeble-minded; he passes muster in the large social
life of the community and barring accidents that nobody can avoid, succeeds in being fairly safe, prosperous and happy.

Therefore in mind at least, there is a close kin
between the so-called normal and the mentally defective. It is a kin that readily removes all repugnance from the minds of those who live with these
unfortunates. For very soon teachers of the defectives see in them all the virtues and all the foibles in germ, at least, which pass with such a brave
show in the real world, and they find themselves not
transported to an entirely new existence, but simply
removed to stage-land wherein the tragedies of the
larger world appear in the burlesques of Punch and

Judy, real to the players as Punch is to children, where the sorrows of life are poignant with the anguish of the moment and as ephemeral as the tears that wash away their sting forever. One knows not whether to laugh or weep when he sees a strong man, forty years old, stand up against a door and bawl like a baby because he could not go down to his beloved laundry work on account of a quarantine for measles, and to hear the attendant say, "Why, Billy Moore, aren't you ashamed to stand up there before everybody and cry like that?" But he was not ashamed and bellowed out his woe with the abandon of a healthy three-year-old who had dropped his candy in the dust.

Summary.—These, in brief, are the physical and mental signs of permanent backwardness. The method of discovering and measuring them has been outlined in this very brief account, but it is detailed enough to enable the teacher or the parent to distinguish temporary backwardness from permanent backwardness. The importance of this ability appears when it is remembered that by the most conservative estimates, about six hundred thousand or seven hundred thousand feeble-minded children are to be found among the eighteen million in the public schools; and of these about ninety thousand are institutional cases, some of them very low indeed in mentality. To distinguish these six hundred thousand from the rest of the six million who are retarded only temporarily is of the highest importance.

Otherwise confusion results in injury and waste and begets in the teacher a skepticism and hopelessness regarding methods of teaching backward children, methods which should never be applied to the feeble-minded who can not be taught some lessons by any method known to man.

CHAPTER IX

THE TEACHER'S DIAGNOSIS

IT IS said that when a new student came for training under the great Agassiz he was given a fish by the master and told to sit down and "look at zee fish!" In a couple of hours he might be asked for a report, would render it and ask what next. "Look at zee fish!" was the invariable answer repeated often for days and even weeks before this master-observer who said "Learn from nature, not books!" was ready to let the tyro begin more ambitious work. If an ordinary fish was worthy of all that observation how much more should the same patient observation be due from the teacher to the special pupil! He is the most wonderful creation in all the world, the epitome of all the limitless past and possessing besides something new that defies all traditional methods and principles of teaching. What that peculiarity is which will henceforth take its place in the creative evolution of the future world, can be found only by the closest, most systematic and thorough observation by the teacher.

Yet how hard it is to see a child! He is such a wild shy creature, untamed, undomesticated and unused to the ways of society. One must steal upon him unawares and watch him in his native habitat to see him as he really is. Among adults he is in captivity. Only in unrestricted play does he reveal his true nature. Under the teacher's eye he is likely to try to be something different from what he is. That is the first difficulty. Then there is the social inheritance of the child showing itself obviously in his clothes, his manners and the care of his body. Through these veils we find ourselves peering back into his home and into his parentage, and being affected in our estimate of his mentality by these draperies that cling so closely to him.

One day a teacher brought two of her pupils to a clinic. They were both girls about ten years of age. Both were backward and in the ungraded class. The teacher was clear in her conviction that Claire was far superior in her mentality to Meg.

Claire was a sweet child. Her presence breathed sainthood. Her fellow pupils had nicknamed her "St. Anne." Her hair was smooth and glossy and the ribbon that held it back from her brow was stiff and new; her gray checkered coat was new; her dark blue dress was of good material and without a spot or blemish or extra wrinkle; her shoes were polished; around her wrists and neck she wore bits of white lace, and a locket hung on her bosom from its gold chain. Her skin was clear and white and her large, violet, sadly-solemn eyes looked out from her oval face, with the heavenly look of a medieval Madonna. Sanctity warmed with amiability, and passivity tempered with docility radiated from the personality of this quiet little girl and immediately enlisted the sympathy of every one who came into her presence.

Meg was the extreme opposite of the saintly Claire. She was a brunette, a vigorous intense one; eyes deep-set and gleaming out from under her shock of cropped straight hair that came down on her low forehead to her straight heavy eyebrows. Her clothes were poor, ill-fitting, old, dirty. Her dress was black, bare of cuffs or collar; her shoes were worn and scarred; her appearance was unrelieved by ornament; her personality expressive of energy shot forth in nervous jets of temper verging on rebellion. To look at her gave one the feeling of approaching a spiny creature, of walking on broken jagged glass.

When the cold hard tests of science were applied to measure the mentality of these two girls it was found that Meg was decidedly the better. Her future was the more promising. She had in her undeveloped potentialities, germs of capabilities that could be trained into serviceable activities. Her energies needed harnessing and directing. Claire had no hidden resources. She was good because she was not bad; not because she overcame evil with good. She had nothing in her. Her appearance was due to well-to-do parents, especially to a painstaking mother. Meg had no mother. She lived with an aunt. She had to dress herself and also two of her small cousins and to do some housework to pay for her living. When she had time she played in the streets. Contrasts between these two girls were due to accidents and incidents; accidents of social inheritance and environment; and inherited qualities like complexion, features and temperaments which were mere incidents to learning.

Obviously the teacher in charge of these two girls did not see these girls as pupils. She did not look through the exteriors and see behind the veil of clothes and manners, through her own conventions and preperceptions into the minimum essentials of her teaching. Those essentials for the teacher were, first, the powers or processes of the mind, inborn or developed, which were already there; and secondly, the potentialities that might yet be developed. These and only these were important to her. The clothes, manners, homes, and other accessories, were merely so many signs of the presence or absence of the essentials. The discovery and measurement of these potentialities is a mental diagnosis, described in the last chapter. The study of mental process is now the task of the teacher and she may well begin it by finding out something of the mental content in the minds she is expected to teach.

Mental Content.—The first thing a teacher should discover about a backward child is how much he knows. Some backward children are marvels of brilliancy in some respects and utterly incapable in others. Their mental defect is not general but special and peculiar, showing itself in total ignorance of only certain branches, and it must be studied thoroughly by the teacher before she can proceed. Mathematical and musical prodigies are frequently utterly unlearned in other sciences. A young man recently died in an asylum, who in some respects was a prodigy of learning and a genius in intellect. He could recite whole pages from Shakespeare, Milton or other classic writers after he had once heard them recited on the stage or elsewhere. Yet he was utterly deficient in other branches of learning, and it was even doubtful if he could read. One of the finest wood-model makers in the world is in an institution for feeble-minded in England. He received a prize for a perfect and complete model of the *Great Eastern,* every mast, spar, rope, block and bit of furniture of which is faithfully reproduced, all requiring the use of about a million one hundred and twenty-five thousand pegs which he himself fashioned on a machine of his own invention. These are a few striking examples of what are encountered in less exaggerated forms every term in any special class. The same extreme irregularities and mental defects may not occur, but large and sometimes surprising deficiencies are discovered by a systematic examination.

How perfectly ridiculous it would be to teach memory-gems to the genius in classics and manual training to the model-maker! And how equally futile it would be to reverse the order of subjects and start the classical genius in manual training with the *Great Eastern* and the model-maker with Milton's *Paradise Lost!*

The content of a pupil's mind must be measured, first, to avoid the obvious waste of learning what is old; and secondly, for the less obvious necessity involved in learning anything new. All learning is leavening. The leaven transmits the fresh dough into a substance similar to itself. In learning we call the process "assimilation of knowledge," and the leaven the "apperceptive mass." The new knowledge must be assimilable. An ordinary child can no more get an idea from the word "chimera" than leaven can leaven a stone. "Chimera" must first be translated into "lion's head" and "goat's body" before he will understand, and then only if he knows what a lion's head and a goat's body are like.

The first and most obvious method of finding what is in a child's mind is to ask him. It requires natural tact and much skill, but it would seem to be an essential part and art of teaching to do it. The ordinary daily review of yesterday's lesson is one method. School examinations should give a systematic, accurate and fairly complete account of the pupil's knowledge of school subjects but they fail to give any estimate of what a child knows about common things, and they do not prove that he has a clear idea because he uses the proper words in a correct answer.

The Child's Interests.—The teacher may approach the pupil with this thought in her mind, "How shall I interest him in the lesson?" or, with the antipodal query, "In what is this pupil interested?" The former attitude is that of the mother who brought her nine-year-old boy to a specialist who found him apparently a ruddy, healthy, normal-minded boy in every way. The specialist finally inquired why she had brought him, and was amazed to hear that the mother held the gravest fears for her son's future because she had discovered, though it nearly broke her heart to say it, that he was a degenerate! The specialist, dumfounded for the moment, asked the agitated woman her reasons for such a terrible suspicion. Then she related how she herself was trying to educate her boy by an ideal method which would inculcate in him an early love for the true, the good and the beautiful. Part of his education consisted of daily visits to a museum near his home, where there was a magnificent collection of the choicest paintings from the best masters. Here she endeavored to instil estheticism into her boy by having him sit quietly in the art-rooms, a different one each day, and absorb art. But, and here the poor woman almost broke down in her anguish, the boy seemed utterly indifferent to the beauty round about him and completely immune to that method of esthetic infection. Instead of silently devouring the masterpieces, he would grow restless, beg her to go, would pull at her skirts, and by every artifice he knew would try to inveigle her to the cases where the swords, daggers, spears, guns and other weapons were kept, where he would stand for hours feasting his eyes on these instruments of blood and destruction. It took all the skill of the expert to convince that good woman that her boy was entirely normal and that he was merely passing through a periodic instinctive stage of his life.

To that woman it was a revelation to find that children were naturally interested in certain objects and certain subjects at certain ages, and that she was attempting the impossible when she was trying to inject into him certain feelings which were not yet there. Of course, this mother knew, as every one else does, that there are great permanent instincts in human beings that run through their whole lives. The aversion to pain and desire for pleasure are two such fundamental feelings. Without them it would be impossible to build any education or to enforce any discipline. Imitation is another wide-spreading instinct. Its roots lie in gregariousness which makes people flock together. The first instinct ornaments and embellishes with morality, patriotism, religion, custom and art what the second founds. Many more of the same kind might be mentioned but they are not important for the teacher, who, in her analysis of a single child, can take their existence for granted. The fact that some, indeed many, instincts are universal and permanent must not obscure the fact that many are also transitory.

By transitory we mean that certain consuming interests of a child's life will rise to a climax, claim all of his attention and fire all of his plans, and then die down and disappear quite naturally and without any external aid or suppression from any one. To diagnose such a case and to know when the infection with a certain set of instincts has taken place, to follow them in their period incubation, and to seize their power when they reach their climax and bind this flood-tide of power to some subject which will be then learned so as never again to be forgotten, demands the genius and skill of a great teacher. If the lesson is thrust on the child too early it may not take, and what is worse, it may render him immune to any later infection by the same subject; if the lesson is delayed it will fall listlessly on a mind whose interest in it is as sear and dead as the autumn leaf. Most anxiously then should the dominant instinct of any child be sought in the teacher's diagnosis.

The instinctive life of children changes from individual to individual. They do not all have the same instincts, and they do not all have them in the same intensity. Nothing is more common than that if we only stop to think of it. It makes the fundamental differences in people, in their characters and in their professions, in all the little incidents and traits that go to differentiate one individual from another. Inborn differences take one boy from the farm and make him a rover of the seas, another a student, another a mechanic, while other differences make him the keeper of the old homestead and the tiller of the soil. One boy has the fighting instinct in him and will work hard in a contest; another lacks it and will do his best when alone. These primary interests manifesting themselves in the impulses of childhood, the tastes of individuals, the foibles and crotchets of children, must be all considered when the special teacher is undertaking the training of a child who has failed in the regular grades where uniformity has been the rule. Perhaps in any one of these impulses she may find the key to unlock the child's mind and thus make him a scholar.

Some scientists believe that the change of instinctive life follows a law. Instincts seem to come and go in periods. These periods are thought to follow and repeat the social history of the race in its climb from savagery to civilization. Therefore it need surprise no one to find that a boy is a little savage or a barbarian in his tastes and interests. Whether this theory is true or not need not concern the teacher, except as it again suggests study to find in what particular period any particular child is at the time she receives him, and as it emphasizes the fact that not all instincts are permanent and fixed.

To summarize, instincts are permanent or transient, universal and particular. They vary from individual to individual, and they vary from time to time in the same individual. These variations seem to follow a periodic law that leads the child to reiterate the history of the race.

A General Instinct.—Play is an instinct so widely diffused that healthy children are lost in it from the time their eyes open in the morning until their heavy lids fall like shadows of the evening. All children play, play when they are let loose from factories and when their bloodless muscles seem incapable of any more exertions. Sad it is to see them; as sad as to see the momentary brightening of a sick child when its dear familiar toys are brought to its bedside, perhaps for the last time. Play is a stimulant when all the doctor's lore fails and his medicines lose their potency. For children are like Juvenal's ancient Romans who cared for nothing except bread and games; and sometimes they are so ardent for it that they imitate Voltaire's French who "omitted the *panem*"—bread—because of the heart-of-hearts' truth that play is the realest world the child will ever find in his earthly seeking. Wise indeed is the teacher who dares to follow Locke's advice and to make everything that children have to do sport and play. For the special class, without doubt, all tasks must be games and all lessons stories; one the play of muscles, the other the play of minds. To be sure that this will not be misunderstood by those who have never entered, or having entered have forgotten, this portion of heaven, let me say that play is not amusement, not even pleasure alone, but the outpouring of all one's strength to accomplish what one desires with all his might. Once in a while a teacher's attention is arrested by a harmony in her schoolroom, when the spirit of work prevails in it and all the air is freighted with spontaneous activity, when every head is bent over book or paper, and the hum of labor is as the humming of bees in the blooming willow-trees in spring. Three summers ago I stepped for a minute into a manual-training class where eighteen pupils were all busy, each one making a different article, while the teacher was sitting silently by the window. All were at play. She had achieved the play-spirit in a class-exercise and it was a perfect schoolroom.

Some Particular Instincts.—Not only do great chains of similar likes and dislikes run through mankind, some to bind individuals together, and some to form common links between young and old, all of which exhibit themselves in the presence of a variety of objects, but there are also particular interests that are aroused only on the presentation of their own peculiar stimulations. Here is a profuseness of innate interests among which we can find inspirers of interest for every variety of study conceivable. Yet how frequently do we hear a teacher say she "has exhausted every effort to arouse some torpid pupil!" Surely, she must mean that she has exhausted her own stock of knowledge on particular instincts, or else her own ingenuity for bringing lessons within striking distance of these highly charged motives to endeavor. For the instincts themselves are innumerable and each one of them can be aroused by an indefinite number of objects. To illustrate merely what they are, let us take hunger. It is present in all children above idiots. The sight of food will always arouse a hungry child and the sight of sweets nearly always any child. Fire is another interesting object, one which through many, many generations of sylvan tribes has bound itself up with the nervous systems of our race so that its leaping flames and glowing embers have in them a weirdness sure to strike an answering note in children. They all like to play with fire. Water,—where must mothers always look for their runaway boys if a river or lake is near? Mud or clay has its own particular charm. Trees call forth an answering challenge to boys when their apish instincts are ripe. Stones to throw are nearer to nature than their cousins, balls. Food, water, earth, trees, sticks, stones, all these *commonest* objects of life are the ones that dwell nearest the depths of children's souls and answer to the call of hidden and mysterious forces in them. These

then should become the paraphernalia of the schoolroom, the quiver of the teacher who is armed for
every emergency. Out of them can be and ought
to be fabricated literally numberless toys and instruments for developing and modifying the primitive traits which must be softened down and
smoothed to fit the modern civilized world.

Temperaments.—Closely allied to instincts are
emotions or feelings. Nothing about a child is
more changeable than his humors. Smiles and tears
chase one another across his face like storm and
sunshine across April skies. Yet it is true that each
possesses a general disposition toward one humor
or another and that we will call his temperament.

About temperament in the ordinary schoolroom,
we know but little and reckon with less. The
reason is obvious. The system fits the average child
and no room is left for consideration of special
tempers or temperaments. But the special class is
"special" for "special" children, and here temperament becomes of mighty importance. Where the
ordinary teacher notes it incidentally, or hears of it
from the anxious mother visiting the school for the
sole purpose of impressing the fact of X's peculiar
"temperament" on the weary schoolmistress who
considers her duty well done when she suppresses
the same peculiarity, the special-class teacher studies
it with care and skill and into each pupil's temperament she will fit herself and her methods of en-
couragement or suppression. Possibly as good a

description of the various temperaments as can be found is the well-worn one of sanguine, melancholy, choleric and phlegmatic, with the combinations that may arise from tinctures of these being mixed in the same child. The first is the hopeful child always bobbing up with great promises of the future, hard to be made to see the need of present persistent application and needing almost constant suppression. His melancholy brother is just the opposite. He must be guarded from criticism as a tender plant from a hail-storm. He grows in the sunshine of praise. The choleric boy is the hard one to manage for his temper flares up in a moment. "Coolness! coolness! coolness!" is the constant exhortation to him. The phlegmatic boy is hard to move by praise or blame, hard to excite, hard to impress and readily acquires a reputation for impenetrable laziness. Usually he is good-natured about it all and often has a knack of sticking to a task that demonstrates afresh the fable of the master-phlegmatic tortoise and the hare. These temperamental differences are really the ones emphasized by parents when they aver that "none of their children are alike." They make a brave attempt under the guise of justice, to treat each child alike no matter if he is entirely different from the rest. Their zealous though mistaken attempts are sometimes softened with charity and much love, but seldom with enough of either. They should temper them even more with the thought that the tempera-

ment of the child comes direct from his parents, a
thing inherited with his nose and eyes and color of
his hair. The special teacher of the backward child
must recognize the differences and must adjust herself to them with all the exhilarating freedom of
individual teaching.

The significance of temperament for the teacher
is seen in the fact that people think as they feel.
"White" suggests orange-blossoms or tombstones,
according to the feeling of the hearer. "It snows!"
brings a "Hurrah" from the healthy boy; a "Dear,
how lucky" from the pleasure-seeking belle; an "Oh,
God!" from the heavy-laden widow. All these
ideas came from "It snows!"; each one came in
answer to the feeling of the subject. If the person
is melancholy, sanguine, choleric or phlegmatic, his
associations of ideas will be more or less directed
by this temperament; he will see things in his environment congruous with it; and he will remember
harmoniously with it. A study of temperament is,
therefore, part of a teacher's diagnosis.

The Perceptive Processes.—Once she has
found what a pupil is primarily and most constantly
interested in, the teacher is ready for her next question, "How does he learn—by eye, ear, or hand?"
Some children learn chiefly through their eyes and
are called visual types. They must see a thing and
then they recall the picture of it in their minds. Others learn by ear, or are auditory types. They must be
told and recall what they remember by hearing it.

Some are kinesthetic, or motor types. They seize upon their knowledge chiefly with their hands and store it up in their muscles and motor-nervous mechanism. Absolutely pure types of any one of the three enumerated are almost never found. Children learn through the eye, ear, nose, mouth, hand and body muscles; but it often happens that a child is predominatingly one type or the other and a teacher succeeds marvelously by studying which faculty is dominant and working accordingly.

Examples of each kind of child show how the neglect of this simple fact of innate differences in perceiving and remembering has led to more than one tragic ending of a child's school career. Instead I will confine myself to a brief statement of some few facts that have been collected by Doctor Elmer E. Jones, which, quite in harmony with the very recent study of personal difference in the inborn capacities of children, illustrate this special sense-difference. Thirty-six pupils in the eighth grade of a public school were permitted to look at ten familiar objects for a second and a half and then were asked to recall what they had seen. The divergencies in the results were amazing. The lowest record was two and six-tenths and the highest seven and four-tenths; that is, children assigned the same lessons and expected to learn them by the same methods varied nearly threefold in their capacities to perceive quickly and accurately, and to recall faithfully the things they saw. Such a test feasible in any schoolroom with the simplest kind of apparatus, will tell with fair certainty whether a child is a visualizer or not.

The same thirty-six children were tested for their auditory memory. Ten lists of names of common objects were read to the class and each one was to write down what he remembered. The lowest record averaged three and a half and the highest nine and seven-tenths, showing that some children possessed nearly three times the power to receive and to recall auditory stimulations that the others had. While the experiments did not show that good visualizers were necessarily good auditors, nor vice versa, they did seem to show that children early form the habit of learning chiefly by ear or by eye.

Another group of children was given each a certain sound and asked immediately to respond to it by a specified act. This test measured power of attention, fatigue, quickness of reaction, and other qualities. Again the greatest differences came out. Some reacted three and a half times faster than others; some were slow and regular; some rapid, but unreliable. Is it necessary to add the obvious that each child should have the lesson presented to him so that he can apprehend it in the easiest and quickest way? One must read it with his own eyes; another must hear it from some one else; another must write it out. Usually, since each child is a mixture of the three types, each child should receive the lesson by eye, ear and hand whenever that is possible. It certainly is safe to say that all the children should not be compelled to learn the lesson one way, and one way only.

Intellectual, Emotional and Volitional Children.—Closely allied to this division made according to perceptive methods is another which rests on the dominance or frequency of one of the three great processes in the mental life of the child, thinking, feeling or willing. The effects of these predominances on teaching and the method of discovering to which type a pupil belongs is indicated in the following illustration.

A teacher held up an orange before her class and watched the effect on them as she went on talking about it. Henry, a rather cold, languid, triangular-faced lad, gave a glance at it and then seemed to pay no more attention to it. The anxious teacher was somewhat irritated by his apparent indifference to her well-planned object-lesson, but she went on asking questions and discussing the orange. Suddenly she noted by Henry's face that he had reached a question mark in his mind.

"What is it, Henry?"

"Was Luther Burbank the man that made the Burbank potato?" was the unscientific and surprisingly irrelevant question.

A moment's consideration revealed that Henry had traveled by a long train of thought, as long and complex as the philosopher Hobbes' friend who suddenly interjected the apparently trivial question

about the value of a Roman penny into a discussion
of the Crucifixion.   The Crucifixion had suggested
the betrayal; the betrayal, the pieces of money; that,
the Roman penny.   Henry saw the orange, thought
of California or the seedless orange; then of Burbank, then of the potato.   Such a boy belongs to
the intellectual type.   He gets knowledge by thinking things out for himself.   All he needs is a start,
some suggestion or other, and lo, his train of
thought has pulled out of the station on a long and
unknown journey.   He is the student *par excellence*.

In front of him was a little girl who seemed all
interest.

"What do you think of the orange, Mary?"
asked the teacher.

"I got a little baby-brother at home and he likes
oranges and when my mama gives him an orange
he gets his face all smeared with it!" volubly re-
plied the little "mother" and it would be easy to see
the trend of her mind toward feelings, even if she
did not use the word "likes."   Her thoughts are
determined by her emotions, and an orange, the
same object that carried the cold Henry off to California and plunged him deep into science, transported Mary to her home and the treasures there.   If
the teacher wishes ever to lodge an idea so it will remain in Mary's mind, she must surround it, over-
lay it and hedge it in with emotional associations;
for Mary represents the emotional type.   Her reading should tell stories of human pathos, her writing

should be letters to folks at home; and her arithmetic must figure how the poor widow can buy clothes for her four children on the pittance she earns. We can not hope for text-books to suit every type of child, but we can hope for teachers who will diagnose their children and will have ingenuity enough to fit their teaching to each disposition.

While the teacher was asking these questions, Tommy, the chubby, freckle-faced, red-haired boy who had to sit on the front seat where the teacher could watch him, was nearly wriggling himself to pieces. He could hardly keep his seat under the almost irresistible impulse to grab the orange in both hands. Every time the teacher raised it, his hands involuntarily went up too, ready to catch it.

"Well, Tommy," at last said the teacher, "what are you bursting to say?"

"I climbed the tree and shook the apples down, last summer, in the country, and the limb broke," he exploded in a breath. Action, vigorous action all the way through; his mind explodes; his sentences shoot out promiscuously and illogically; his thoughts are all dynamic with motion. He wants to seize the orange, handle it, toss it up in the air, climb the tree it grew on. Whatever lessons the teacher wants him to learn must be full of action, learned by writing them on the blackboard, if possible, where plenty of movement is necessary, or by walking, or beating time, or in any way that will lodge the thing to be learned in his muscles.

His chief organ of apprehension is his hand and he will take and hold what he can get his hands on.

These three children are extreme types. The rest of the class were not so pronounced. They were mixtures of these, partly intellectual, partly emotional, partly volitional. It demands a closer observation to bring out which process dominated with them, but it can be done by simple expedients similar to the presentation of the orange. Elaborate tests are useful and have their places, but no teacher need wait for an inventor to formulate them, nor an expert to apply them. When her eyes are once open to such typical differences in pupils, the Henrys, Marys and Tommies thrust themselves on her attention. From these exceptional children often come the backward pupils who can learn by only one method.

The Intellectual Processes.—When a child sees "c-a-t" and can from those letters gain the knowledge "cat" he has used all the mental processes given to a human being. This is true for the simplest bit of knowledge one can imagine. The more complex acquisitions are but repetitions of these simpler processes in which many processes once conscious are now unconscious habits. Mental ability of a high order, then, depends on the rapidity and accuracy with which this simple and unitary process of knowing is performed and on the ease and rapidity with which it becomes habitual with regard to certain objects and certain processes.

Any observer can get a glimpse of this truth by noting how exceedingly difficult is the first step of a baby, or the first word written by a pupil, and how exceedingly easy are the most complex and intricate intellectual operations to one who has practised them until he has reduced a large part of the operation to mere habit. The real conscious acquisition of knowledge, the real "learning process" is therefore unitary and can not, strictly speaking, be separated into parts. Certain phases of it can be attended to by an observer, and these phases can be named perception, memory, imagination and reason, or any other convenient terms, and can then be considered separately. The teacher, however, need not carry this analysis so far and treat it so seriously as to believe that certain studies will involve only certain of these parts and not other parts. It may be somewhat difficult to see reasoning in consciously securing the idea cat from "c-a-t," but a little thought will convince any one that the one who recognizes it as such must see that it is similar or dissimilar to many other symbols. It is similar to the symbol he studied yesterday; therefore, it is "cat" to-day, is the reasoning involved and made explicit. Mathematics, which is a shorthand language, makes this reasoning process, usually unconscious, prominent and noticeable. It therefore is said to train the reason.

An analysis of these higher intellectual processes, while not important in themselves to the teacher, is of enormous importance when applied to the art of her profession. We have already seen that certain children belong to certain types because of their methods of perceiving. The same classification also applies to memory. If a child must see an object in order to know it, he will then be almost certain to recall it by seeing a visual memory-image of it. If he can do that easily and quickly he will probably make a good scholar; for learning by eye and recalling what is learned are the chief requirements of schools and colleges as now conducted. If he must hear what he learns, he will recall the sound of it. As this method is not so prevalent for giving knowledge he may be handicapped somewhat. But the sorest trial is reserved for the motor-type pupil who must handle things to know them, or must write words to grasp ideas, and must express what he knows in action. Though he may make the sure scholar he is usually slower and easily falls into the backward class of pupils.

Further, memory itself can be analyzed into certain phases. To say that a child has a poor memory is not at all sufficient; and to say that he has a poor visual memory is not enough. Possibly the trouble lies in his vague perceptions due to some physical defect of the eyes. When the lesson is presented to him properly he has no trouble with his memory. Possibly the lesson does not interest him and it should be connected more closely with his dominant instincts. Then, when we come to memory proper, possibly he can not *retain* what he learns; possibly he can not *recall* it at the proper time; possibly he can not *recognize* it when it is recalled. These subsidiary parts of the process of memory are so closely related that just as with the great processes of consciousness, they can not be disentangled except for consideration and for correction in pupils with poor memories.

This discussion leads us to the training of the memory. With so much popular information on the subject, it may be difficult to say anything that is not already known. First, it should be noted that we have the simple, natural physiological memory which acts seemingly automatically in recording an object, retaining it till we wish to have it again, recalling it and recognizing it. Such a memory is an innate power and it can not be increased by any amount of training. Whatever one gains in one direction he loses in another. Secondly, we have also a memory organized according to certain laws of association, which can be trained to remember certain facts which we now habitually forget. That is done by consciously forming links of association between the items to be remembered. These links must be formed according to the laws of memory, the first and most general of which is the law of contiguity, according to which law things occurring in the mind together once, tend to come back together when one of them is recalled. Horse and wagon, house and yard, father and mother, are joined by such tendencies. When one term is mentioned the one that comes back out of the many that are possible, will be determined to some extent by other laws. If one says "teeth" the *habit* of toothbrushing may make one think of brush; if this morning he bought some new tooth-powder, *recency* may make him think of that; if yesterday he had a painful molar filled, *intensity* may make him think of that; if he is *feeling* particularly bad, senility and death may come to him through the intermediate thought of the loss of his teeth. A special emotion, like a permanent temperamental disposition, will affect the train of association and memory. To train the memory one must go over and over a lesson; or he must connect it so vitally with his interests or instincts that one impression is an ineradicable one because of its intensity; or he must review it just before he wants it; or he must learn those things congruent with his mood.

Some of these requirements are more readily brought under control than others. Repetition is almost the sole method of training the memory, or of learning, in the schoolroom. Sometimes intense experiences are associated with the thing to be learned by punishments or rewards. Recency of experience is insisted on by demanding a review of the lesson just before coming to class. Feelings are given only an indirect and small part in the matter.

Of the associations under control the easiest to

use for memory-training are associations by similarity and dissimilarity. The range of these two relations is very, very wide, running through all the different senses, affecting sights and sounds, pains and pleasures, emotions and ideas. It seems so easy to remember things that are like something we already know, or opposite to what we know. Anywhere we meet the date 1492, no matter in what history, it is an old friend readily taken into the family of facts we already have. "Tom Campbell burned natural gas at Barcelona Harbor," is full of similarities for me. The man's name is associated with what our old school-bell used to say to us years ago; "b" in bell and burn is enough to remind me of burning the natural gas; "bar" and "har" enough to locate the place. The schemes that have been worked out are almost infinite in number and variety, but they all base their claims for usefulness on the laws of association, especially the last two. These two form the foundation for all reasoning.

At first sight the statement that reasoning and conscious, deliberate association by similarity are the same, may sound strange, but I am sure that a little reflection by any one will give enough knowledge on the subject to cover his needs in analyzing the mental processes of a pupil. The difference between the association by similarity in memory and in reasoning comes from the fact that in memory it leads to facts already known and in reasoning it leads to truths not yet known. In reasoning it amounts practically to imagination with imagination putting together ideas in new forms instead of putting things together in new forms, and putting them together because they are similar rather than for any other purpose. Thus it is seen how easily the higher processes of the mind merge together so closely that they defy analysis. It is enough for the teacher to note the processes of perception and of memory and to study these in each pupil. If she does that well she will be able to suit her instruction to the peculiarities of her pupils, which is the end and aim of her diagnosis.

It is of more importance to know what a boy imagines than how he imagines. His imaginings throw light on his interests and reveal the instinctive stage in which he is living. The same is true of his reasonings. Both of them will show the teacher the way to lodge her lessons in his mind. An ingenious teacher can do it, and the way to do it will often be found by diagnosing her pupil.

Happily, in the American schools the individual child and his innate peculiarities are being underscored for an emphasis heretofore only dreamed of but never really hoped for by progressive educators. New tests for measuring not only what is in his mind but also how he perceives, remembers, imagines and reasons are being formulated as rapidly as careful investigation and wide experiment will permit. Already there are many systems ready to put into the hands of the teachers for diagnosing individual children. Both of the emphases, the emphasis upon the individual and the emphasis upon diagnosis, have long been explicit in teaching backward children. They date from the day when Doctor Itard studied the wild-boy of France, and Doctor Seguin set up his first class to teach the mentally defective in 1837. Teachers in institutions for the feeble-minded would not know how to proceed with their teaching without first making or having made a thorough diagnosis of each child. What has been found in these fields to be of so much value will surely yield results when applied to normal children and to temporarily backward children.

CHAPTER X

A COUNTRY girl, a real country girl, as awkward and unsophisticated as the proverbial Liza Ann of fiction or comedy, one day presented herself to a training school for special teachers in a large city. She had grown up on a farm, taught school in a one-room country schoolhouse, heard something about teaching backward children and out of the "invisible ether" came the vision of herself as a special teacher. Forthwith, she began to investigate, found how much it would cost to take the course, saved the exact amount, and one day presented herself to the principal of the training school.

The Teacher.—Needless to say it was a shock to that expert trainer. It all looked so hopeless to her who knew so well the difficulty in that great city of securing positions for the best and most promising graduates, the need of personality, the labor of the training, sometimes the weary waiting after the training was over. She delicately broached the situation to the applicant and was appalled when she heard how little money, and silenced when she

noted how much confidence this raw country girl
had brought with her. There was nothing to do
but enroll her. That was done and the girl took
the course.

When she finished, as fortune would have it, a
call came to the supervisor for a special teacher to
go to an out-of-the-way corner of the city, a mis-
carried subdivision, sterile, frustrated, sparsely
settled, consisting chiefly of the school-building and
scattered frame dwellings with stretches of sand
and weeds between them. Nobody else wanted to
go there. The supervisor thought of the country
graduate and wondered if she dared send *her*. The
principal out there was a friend of hers and she
hated to serve him so, but something had to be
done and the happy country girl was dispatched.

For two weeks the supervisor trembled every time
the telephone bell rang. But no word came from
the suburb. When the silence became no longer
bearable, she took the car and traveled out to the
school. Her friend, the principal, resolutely avoided
reference to the new teacher. At last the supervisor made the plunge. "How-er is Miss C., the
new teacher doing?" she ventured. "Splendidly!
Splendidly!" was the principal's breath-taking re-
joinder. "She's a wonder. When she came we
gave her an empty room and ten boys nobody could
teach or control. She sent those boys out to scour
the country for lumber, tin, nails, tools, string and
everything they needed. They got tools from home,

begged packing-boxes, spent their own money for nails and before long they had that room finished and equipped in a home-made but up-to-date manner and were busy making other articles they wanted. Now we send to her any pupils anybody has any trouble with and she adopts them into the family!"

And to make the truth seem still more like fiction, the country girl's class carried off the prize in that urban school system for the best exhibit of special-class work. This teacher represents both a method of teaching and a type of teacher.

Her Mental Qualifications.—In general there may be said to be two types of teachers: the vital and the mechanical. Of these two the special-class teacher must undoubtedly belong to the former. Many reasons urge to that conclusion. A few are mentioned here and many more will suggest themselves to the reader. First, the teacher's field is comparatively new. The first class ever organized for the deliberate teaching of the mental defectives was taught by Seguin in 1837. For decades afterward such instruction was limited to institutions and unknown to the public schools. Sporadic classes occurred earlier, but the real movement for special classes in public schools did not begin until the nineties of the last century. A score of years would nearly cover their history in this country. The field is hardly more than touched; the methods are experimental; invention and ingenuity have the widest latitude and the most promising opportunities in this educational realm. The teacher must be of the vital, wide-awake, facile, inventive type, eager for improvement and development and constitutionally opposed to routine. Two young women go to a college for specialized training. One fills her avid note-book full of detailed notes. She notes that singing comes at 9:00 A. M. and lasts six and a half minutes on Monday, six on Tuesday; six and a half on Wednesday, etc.; that for clay modeling the children are given wet clay on newspapers; that a pupil spoiled one piece of board and threw it into the waste-basket; that James modeled a turnip by beginning at the bottom; that Harry's chalk scratched horribly on the blackboard and Miss F., the teacher, never seemed to notice it, etc., etc., *ad infinitum*. These illustrations are by no means fanciful but have been culled from teachers' actual notes made on their observation of special-class methods.

On the other hand, here is a young girl from a mountain-town. She sees, observes, notes and queries. "Why does singing come first?" "How can sand be kept moist in a sand board?" "Should boys make toy guns, swords, spears?" "At what age should the children have a garden?" Such a type of mind is bound to get down to the bases of methods and to grasp the principles of teaching. From such inquiring minds have always come the reformers and leaders of the educational world. Probably there is room for both kinds of minds in general teaching; and surely the ideal teacher of the special class will conform to the thinking type.

Secondly, the teacher must always be further preparing herself. She can not stop for a year or a term and rest on the fact that she has years of experience behind her. Experience here does not count for much. Yesterday's experience is supplanted by to-day's discoveries and the yesterday's static teacher is supplanted by to-day's dynamic one.

A third reason is the well-known one that this kind of teacher deals with individuals rather than classes. Her results are not measured in terms of grades, amount of book-space covered, discipline or schoolroom order, but in regenerated lives of boys and girls who came to her hopelessly bad or backward and unfit for regular classes or for regular lives. Her work is wrought on them individually, and by their ability to come back to class and take a new part in school life her efficiency is determined. Her stupid scholars can not be relegated to a backward class and her bad ones must *not* be expelled from school.

Her Physical Attributes.—Because we are so much bound by conventions we seldom think of the physical qualifications for any teacher as after all, *very* vital. We see so many types of women and men, weak and strong, entering the profession, succeeding in it, and working even down to the day of their deaths that we tend to discount robust health as the first requisite for a teacher who lives to teach. Still, it is true that health is a prime essential for any teacher, and this truth is doubly true for the special teacher. Her health must be of that impregnable, unflagging, unfatiguing kind that radiates the joy of living. Headaches, colds, blues, stresses and strains, fits of discouragement, discontent, temper, vague aches and vaguer longings, whims, notions, crotchets, disagreeable personal traits of mind and character, all the little luxuries of life that other people may allow themselves and still succeed must be resolutely forbidden to this teacher. Her daily life must be a poised one; quiet, serene, free from worries and doubts that come from constitutional defects, reigning over her flock with the assured power of personality acting directly and without apparent means. All this must be reflected in her every movement and her every tone. One who has only seen such teachers moving so serenely about the class-room during the day can guess the nervous energy and absolute self-control it requires to keep every motion precisely regulated, every tone perfectly modulated. No matter what sudden catastrophe occurs, whether a degenerate suddenly flies into a rage and slashes his neighbor with a knife or knocks him on the head with a hammer, or two children at once fall down in epileptic fits, the teacher must remain serene. An instant's failure on her part would work havoc on her nervously unstable brood. Only the perfectly healthy woman can be ready for such emergencies.

As to her other physical qualifications, like size, age, looks, etc., they are secondary to healthy poise.

Temperament of the Teacher.—With the abounding health required of the special teacher, it need hardly be said that she must be of a sanguine-phlegmatic temperament. If there is a trace of melancholy in her constitution it will surely develop in the atmosphere of the slow, dull, stupid, oftentimes hopeless, and frequently deformed and afflicted flotsam and jetsam that are cast by the ebb and flow of pedagogical tides upon her hands. Living in such an atmosphere requires the hopeful temperament that can see glimmerings of a bright future in the worst cases and a phlegmatism that will neither wear itself out in useless and ceaseless strivings for the impossible nor fret itself to pieces against the infinite worries of every day. To these qualities of temper must be added a motor disposition; the desire to move about, not hastily nor restlessly but purposively and deliberately; to get things done, to organize, to push forward with a quiet unceasing perseverance. The chief emotional element required is the spirit of kindliness that naturally arises from a healthy body and a willingness to do.

The Teacher's Special Training.—The special fitting of a special teacher for her work should be acquired in a school or college devoted to teaching teachers of public schools rather than one devoted to teaching teachers in institutions for the feeble-minded. That must not be taken to mean that the instruction to teachers in the latter institutions is not efficient nor at all adequate for the work. Such preparation is good, and in certain institutions is certainly far better than the instruction in some universities or normal schools. But, on the whole, the preparation in institutions is calculated to fit teachers best for institution work. Public schools are different. Likewise the whole background of schools and institutions is dissimilar and this often spells the difference between successful and unsuccessful teaching. Besides, as I have already said, the types of children taught, and therefore, the objectives of teaching, are different. Let the young teacher then seek out a school having the best equipment, the longest record of experience in teaching special teachers, one with a special class of special children secured from the public schools, and there let her secure her special training. It should, of course, include all the methods of the special class-room. Much as I have here emphasized diagnosis as a necessary preliminary and eliminator of waste, still the student preparing for teaching must not overemphasize this most fascinating portion of her future work to the exclusion of principles and methods of teaching. Both phases are necessary. The diagnosis is preliminary, comparatively brief, and once done needs not to be repeated. Teaching is the real work; is comparatively lengthy, full of monotony and often discouraging, requiring both skill and character to maintain efficiently and to complete tri-

umphantly. Besides the usual methods of special-
class training she should learn manual work, including bench work in carpentry, basket weaving,
raffia work, clay-modeling, sand-modeling, drawing, water-color work and, what only a few teachers
have yet attempted, enough knowledge of machinery
to take apart a clock, odd bits of household plumb-
ing, faucets, gas-cocks, electric bells, sewing-ma-
chines, phonographs, etc. Such an array of knowledge may seem formidable but she is not through
yet. The expert teacher must add to her other accomplishments the art of physical culture encom-
passing the usual calisthenics, swimming, a number
of indoor and outdoor games, and enough skill to
follow the directions of a physician in corrective
gymnastics. Closely allied to this is speech-training,
which so many of her pupils will need and on
which so much mental development intimately depends. Such demands may seem appalling but they
are entirely reasonable and will in practise be found
little enough. Full proficiency in all of them may
never be acquired. In the beginning only the rudiments need be known. But a preliminary knowledge of many things is essential. A knowledge of
the daily demands of the schoolroom will soon be
transformed into an easy familiarity and a master-
ful skill.

Experience.—Whether she is a young teacher
specially prepared for the work or one from the
regular grades with a long and varied experience

is secondary to the question of vitality. The latter, by reason of age and the mechanizing effect of grade-teaching would more likely be unfitted in this respect than the beginner. However, no rule can be made absolute here. A middle-aged woman with years of experience through every grade of a public school and a young woman with but a few years of teaching to her credit both came from western cities for one summer's training in special-class work in an eastern university and both went back home and made successes of their careers. Preparation is indispensable. This preparation may be gained in the regular grades and supplemented with regular training in some school; or it may be obtained without the regular-class experience. It should, however, be gained in a school or university rather than in an institution for the feeble-minded where, in the first place, only one great class of backward children are met and the methods are not arranged for the purpose of restoring the pupils to society; and, in the second place, where the problems of the public school system are not met at all or, at best, only in a modified form. It would be preferable to choose teachers who grew up in the country rather than those limited to the city life alone. So many of the pedagogical methods are but adaptations to the natural life of children in the country that at least some first-hand experience in country life is as valuable as modes of procedure in the class-room.

The Need of Special-Class Teachers.—A word might be added concerning the need of special teachers and the possibilities of the profession. I fear that I have set the ideals so high and have dwelt so lengthily on the strenuousness and exactingness of the work that it might seem to a young person appalling rather than appealing. A very brief experience would assure any one of the contrary. The evident need of the children, the novelty and freedom of the field, the daily sight of appreciably growing boys and girls, the personal pride generated in each pupil as he responds to the training, the extra recompense in salary, the increasing expansion of the work throughout the world, the constant and unceasing development of the teacher herself, are all factors that make this field of endeavor one of the most fascinating and most cheering to the real teacher aiming to spend her life in good works. All the horror of "abnormal" children perishes with a closer acquaintance with the little people whose only fault is their littleness in mind and often in body. In this Lilliputian world of intellect old standards are quickly adjusted to new conditions, and the "bright," "cheery," "loving," "hard-working," "grateful" children are to be found here just as they are found in any group of children. The terms may take on a relative meaning but they are as real in their content and comfort here as anywhere else. The genuine teacher will soon find herself just as proud of her charges, just as fond of them and with

just as many friends among them as the teacher in
the regular grades. Slow they may always be, needing unlimited patience and giving innumerable
trials; but the person who puts life above livelihood
knows that trials overcome bring patience with a
sense of victory and of life through growth.

The first requisite for holding a special class is
a place in which to hold it. Usually such classes are
organized in schools already established and the location and number of the rooms and the material
equipment are determined largely by the exigencies
of the circumstances. Such should not be the condition. The whole plan and every procedure should
be determined alone by the peculiar needs of the
pupils to be taught. Many of these pupils present
paradoxical mental states. Their attention is the
flightiest and their nerves the most unstable. Yet
their sensibilities are dulled, their perceptions
blunted, their gift of ideation either nil or very weak.
This is true of the mental defectives and partially
true of the temporarily backward. To excite the
liveliest possible sensations, and so produce the most
vivid and lasting perceptions and yet not to over-
stimulate the explosive nervous systems, is one of
the prime and most constant functions of the passive surroundings of these pupils. In the location
and the furnishing of their class-rooms this objective, with others, must be kept always in mind.

The Location of the Rooms.—The first point
of attention is the location of the rooms. They

should not be adjacent to other class-rooms, if possible, since the tramp of physical exercises, the noise of manual work, the sound of music and singing may entirely interfere with other classes. While thus comparatively removed for the sake of quiet to others, the children must equally be protected by location from the noises outside the school building. The side of the building with a favorable exposure for sun and air must be chosen. Some class-rooms have no sashes in the windows but are open to the air continually. Light and sunshine, shade and shadow must all be provided for by proper lighting and proportioned shading with awnings. Heating and ventilation of course must be well observed; as well as that very indefinite but essential quality known as airiness. Easy access to suitable lavatories is another convenience not to be overlooked. In brief, quiet, air, light, space, comfort and convenience, these are cardinal points in the location of the class-rooms. How necessary some of these factors are may be seen from the fact that a whole special class was demoralized by the excitement aroused by taking a flash-light photograph. All class activities had to be suspended for the rest of the day. One child was almost thrown into a fit; and this, too, not from fear, for all of them had been doubly reassured that nothing would hurt them, but from mere nervous tension over the unusual and novel.

The Number of Rooms.—At least three rooms

are needed for a class of fifteen pupils. This comparatively generous number is required partly because the nature of the work demands divisions and subdivisions of the class reaching almost, if not wholly, to individual instruction, though it is not impossible to carry on all the activities involved in one room. One room may be devoted chiefly to manual work and in it all the work-benches, tools and lumber can be stored. Another is devoted chiefly to class work of the usual kind. The other should be reserved for a rest room and possibly physical training, including speech-training. The last exercise must usually be carried on with one pupil at a time and in a room where other sounds are almost wholly eliminated. Besides the rooms, a swimming pool, an outdoor playground, a park, museums, and many points of living interest like factories and shops, are all additional and very helpful advantages. In fact, the equipment for a special class should realize the ideal equipment for any school.

The Furnishings of the Rooms.—Each room should be furnished to suit the children. Pictures, flags, ferns, flowers, aquaria, birds, curios, samples of manufacturing products, all the endless odds and ends that go to make up the complex world about them should be where these children can see and handle the things themselves. They can not read and image as a normal child can; they must see, hear, taste, smell, handle in order to become acquainted with the strange and overwhelmingly complex world about them. Therefore the aim must be to create a replica in microcosm of the world outside the schoolroom where, under direction, without danger and at their leisure, they can become acquainted with things themselves.

Home-Made and Store-Bought Equipment.— Besides furnishings the usual equipment of tools and materials for a complete kindergarten must be furnished. Here, however, a radical departure is sometimes made by most able teachers. Instead of fully furnishing and equipping rooms the children themselves are set to that task. Homely and home-made articles take the place of elaborate manufactured ones. The greatest achievement thus attained is not the objective results in the room, but the effect on the children themselves. To make something from something is something; but to make something from nothing is an achievement supreme. The interest aroused in hunting up soap-boxes, lumber, strings, cord, nails, screws, paints, tools, toys, plants, flowers, sand, clay, shells, pebbles, vegetables, pictures, charts, maps, etc., etc., the use of old things for new purposes, the applications of things on hand to needs, the invention and discovery of means, methods and materials to do things, have a charm and spontaneity, a spirit of Robinson Crusoe adventure that breeds and maintains interest better than the most elaborate equipments. The possibilities of such a procedure and the actualities accomplished in some places ought to deter any new teacher from discouragement over her meager advantages. For those who have the opportunity and face the need a list of tools and materials actually used in special class is appended:

EQUIPMENT

10 ordinary pine-top kitchen tables with drawers, 36 x 23 in. $1.95 each.
20 children's chairs, 12-in. and 14-in. leg. 80 cts. $8.50 per doz.
3 double work-benches, 51 x 22 in. $22.00 (5 drawers).
1 sand tray.
1 couch or cot. $1.50 up.
2 teacher's desks. No. 26,875, 42 x 30 in. $11.50 each with back panel tall top.
Plants for room decoration.
20 steamer chairs. $1.50 and $2.25 with rest for feet; $1.25 and $2.00 without foot-rest.
20 3½-ft. wands. 10 cts. each.
15 pairs of 1-lb. dumb-bells. 45 cts. per pair.
15 pairs of ¾-lb. Indian clubs. 35 cts. pair.
1 Pianola piano.
½ doz. bean bags.
½ ream oaktag paper, 9 x 14.
1 large jar of library paste.
1 medium bottle glue.
½ doz. lead-pencils, hard.

SUPPLIES

Tools:
1 brace. $1.25 to $2.50.
½ doz. bits. 6/32 (30 cts.), ⅛ (30 cts.), ⅜ (35 cts.), ½ (35 cts.), ¾ (45 cts.).
2 fret saws. 25 cts.
6 doz. blades. 15 cts. a doz.

2 varnish brushes (small).

3 chisels. ¼-in. 45 cts.; ½-in. 45 cts.; 1-in. 75 cts.

Brads. ¾ No. 19, 12 cts. a lb.; 1 No. 16, 12 cts. a lb.

Nails. 1¾ No. 12, 8 cts. a lb.

Sandpaper, No. 1. 1 ct. a sheet.

4 planes, smoothing. $1.35.

1 pliers, square nose. 45 cts.

2 steel rulers. About 75 cts.

4 10-in. back saws. $1.35.

1 crosscut. $1.50 to $2.00.

1 rip-saw. $2.25.

1 screw-driver, medium. 30 cts.

Screws. Flat, 1-in. No. 6, 30 cts. gross; 1½-in. No. 10, 35 cts. gross.

4 files, flat, 10-in. 25 cts. each.

1 mallet, round.

1 hammer, claw. 60 cts.

6 hammers, tack. 45 cts.

4 try-squares, 6-in. 30 cts.

1 oil stone. 25 cts.

½ gal. turpentine.

1 can stain, oil walnut. 90 cts. a qt.

25 dowels.

Cane for chairs.

1 lb. fine-fine. 75 cts. bundle.

1 lb. fine. 75 cts. bundle.

1 lb. medium. 75 cts. bundle.

4 lbs. raffia. Light brown, green, 55 cts. lb.; old blue, natural, 25 cts.

1 lb. reed No. 1. $1.25 lb.

1 lb. reed No. 2. 95 cts. lb.

1 lb. reed No. 3. 75 cts. lb.

1 lb. reed No. 5. 55 cts. lb.

1½ doz. scissors, sharp pointed, 5-in. $2.25 doz.

Paper:

12 pkgs. Prang's colored paper, 4 x 4; 20 x 25. 5 cts. sheet, 50 cts. a doz.

Clay:
    50 lbs. clay. 25 cts. a brick (5 lbs.).
    1 jar for clay.

Chalk:
    1 box of white chalk. 35 cts. a gross.
    1 box of colored chalk. 10 cts.

Paints:
    18 boxes of water colors. 25 cts. small; 65 cts.
        large.
    2 doz. water color brushes. 10 cts. each; $1.00
        doz.; No. 3 brush medium.
    2 doz. box grease crayons. 50 cts. doz.

Wood:
    50 basswood planks, ¼ in.
    25 ft. joists, white pine, 1¾ in.
    2 boards, ⅞ white pine, clear dressed.
    2 boards, ⅝ white wood, clear dressed.
    2 boards, ½ white wood, clear dressed.
    15 ft. ⅞ joists, white pine.
    10 ft. pine strips, white, ⅞ in. square, dressed
        four sides.

Courses for Backward Children.—By the very nature of the case strict courses of study are inapplicable to backward children. Many of them are made backward because attempts are made to conform them to courses, and many are cured by the simple expedient of giving them exercises fitted to their needs and capacities. They require individual instruction not only in the sense that they must receive personal attention from the teacher directed to each child individually, but that each one must have studies and methods of teaching those studies adapted to him. With this understanding, namely, that liberal variations should be made from the curricula set down, we can offer a few suggestions to those without a technical training, regarding the day's program and the merest sketch of manual work for the first several grades.

The daily time schedule is one similar to that used in ungraded classes.

DAILY PROGRAM OF SPECIAL CLASS

9:00– 9:15—Opening exercises all together.
9:15– 9:30—Morning talk to all.
9:30– 9:45—Written language.
9:45–10:00—Paper language.
10:00–10:15—Number.
10:15–10:30—Relaxation.
10:30–11:00—Manual work.
11:00–11:30—Reading.
11:30–12:30—Gymnasium and pool.
12:30– 2:00—Luncheon and rest.
2:00– 2:20—Drawing.
2:20– 2:40—Sense training.
2:40– 3:00—Games.
3:00– 3:15—Physical work—all children.
3:15– 3:30—Folk dancing or corrective gymnastics.
3:30– 4:00—Articulation or story dramatization.

As a suggestion for manual work of the simplest kind, the following has been found valuable:

GUIDING PRINCIPLES

1. The purpose of the work should be to develop the children, not merely to produce results in material things. The *progress* a child makes in comparison with his first efforts is far more significant than his

output. His interest, attention, perseverance, ingenuity are factors of the greatest moment.

2. The lessons given below are designed to suit the capacities of children of different ages, and approximately also arranged to appeal to their instinctive life-stages.

3. The materials used should be, as far as possible, those found in the neighborhood. What to make, out of what to make it, where to secure the material for making it, are questions often opening up more educational processes than actually making the thing itself.

For Children From Five Years to Eight Years

1. Bead-stringing, using small fruits like haw-apples, and seeds, combined to form effective color-designs.

2. Paper boxes. A multitude of forms will occur to any mind.

3. Paper-weaving, mats, baskets, book-marks. Willow-twigs, grasses, long pine needles, etc., can also be used.

4. Card-board work. All kinds of models; animals, birds, fish, weapons for boys, Indian life, pioneer life, colonial life, boats, toys. Nearly everything possible to make with cards can also be made with burs from common burdock, and many things can be made from leaves.

5. Clay-modeling. The clay can be procured by the children. Sometimes different colors are found in the same locality. Clay provides a most excellent medium for developing children's perseverance, for it can be rekneaded and reshaped again and again until an effect is produced. An infinite variety of objects can be made. Let the children follow their own fancies.

6. Sand piles. Let fancy, instinct, utility and art dictate what shall be made.

7. Permit the children to take apart and examine

every common article possible, like puzzles, faucets, coffee-mills, pumps, clocks, model stoves, steam-engines, etc., etc.

Children From Nine Years to Twelve Years

1. The same kind of work as that given to the lower grades but more advanced in detail, exactness, intricacy and beauty can be given.

2. With the various materials required,—cardboard, wood, clay, cement and stone,—make models each of the typical industries of the neighborhood. This can be carried out in as much detail as the most advanced pupil desires. For example, farming requires barns, stables, animals, fowls, wagons, machinery, trees, streams, etc.

3. With the materials required make toys suitable for play and games appropriate for children's ages. Bats, oars, sleds, skees, clubs, spears, bows, swords, guns, dolls, doll-clothes, clay-dishes, etc.

4. Weaving grape-vines, corn-husks, rye-straw, willow, reed, raffia, carpet-rags, cane, etc.

For Children From Thirteen Years to Fifteen Years—Constructive and Useful

GROUP	PROCESSES	PROJECTS
1. Laying out and sawing.	Gaging, knife-lining, sawing, testing with trysquare, nailing, stock machine—planed or rough. (Use box boards.)	Crate, bench-hook, bird-house, planting box, chicken-coop, box-trap, shelves, feed trough, tomato trellis.
2. Free planing.	Adjustment, care and use of jack plane. No definite dimensions.	Cutting board, ropewind, breeding-cage, rootcage, stringwinder for the garden line, swing-board, shelves, wood specimens, saltbox, feed-box, plant-markers, negative-rack.
3. Accurate planing.	Planing true surfaces *to dimensions.* Test for trueness and squareness.	Spool-holder, ringtoss, game-board, winding-sticks, hat-rack, stirring-stick.
4. Chiseling.	Use of chisel in vertical position to produce convex surface by tangents. Lap-joint, bridle-joint, Boring, paring.	Funnel-rack, broom-holder, windmill, sawbuck, tool-rack, Christmas tree holder, window-screen, milking-stool, mirror apparatus, wall-rack.
5. Simple modeling.	Use of turning saw and spoke-shave, sandpaper.	Sleeve-board, breadboard, coathangers, calendar back, stirring paddle, sled, book-rack, netneedle, camp-stool.

For Children From Thirteen Years to Fifteen Years—Constructive and Useful

GROUP	PROCESSES	PROJECTS
6. Simple construction.	Fastening parts together with nails, screws accurately.	Nail-box, knife-box, polishing-box, broom-holder, dog-kennel, book-rack, balance plate-rack, hand-loom, water-wheel, footstool, mag-azine-rack, trestle, snow-plow, tab-oret, T-square.
7. Simple joinery.	Cross-lap joint, groove joint, miter joint, bridle joint.	Window-box, ventilator, book-rack, necktie-rack, magazine-rack, foot-stool, wall-rack, octagonal taboret, pedestal, picture framing, fireless cooker, rafter-model, stairs model, hurdle.
8. Glue joint.	Joint planing, use of glue.	Tea table, magazine stand, folding screen, drawing board.
9. Mortise and tenon joint.	Lay-out, cutting mortise, cutting, tenon, fastening.	Umbrella-stand, taboret, book-trough, piano-bench, stool, chair, reading-table.

INDEX

INDEX

The Childhood and Youth Series

THE Childhood and Youth Series is the first systematic attempt to give to parents, teachers, social workers and all others interested in the care and training of the young, the best modern knowledge about children in a manner easily understood and thoroughly interesting. The various volumes present in popular style the results of research in every phase of child-life, every topic being handled with strict scientific accuracy, but at the same time in a simple, concrete and practical way.

Special emphasis is laid on the everyday problems arising in the activities of the home and school, the street and places of work and amusement. Each subject is discussed by a prominent authority, competent to deal with it alike in its scientific and practical aspects. It has been constantly borne in mind by the author of each volume that the Childhood and Youth Series is intended primarily as a guide for parents and teachers.

Much of the literature that we have had in the past dealing with such subjects has had no popular appeal or application. It has been dry, technical and unintelligible for the average mother —uninteresting to her, at least. The Childhood and Youth Series, however, is not academic in any respect; it is intimate and confidential, the authors taking the attitude of friends and advisers and their style having all the characteristics of convincing heart-to-heart talks. If they are always scientific, they are also always sympathetic.

In the general field of the child's welfare and progress in mind, body and emotions, the practical results of the latest scientific study are set forth in clear and graphic form.

Questions of many and widely varying kinds are considered —questions which come up every day in the home and in the school and which parents and teachers find it difficult to answer. The problems of food, nutrition, hygiene, physical defects and

The Childhood and Youth Series

deficiencies, nerves and nervous energy, sleep, stimulants and narcotics, etc., receive careful treatment. The intellectual phases are considered in other volumes, devoted to perception, memory, reason and the imagination. Such emotions as fear, anger, pride, shame and the like are adequately treated.

In matters that have to do with the child's moral and social well-being, all the latest theories are tested and explained. The causes and prevention of juvenile delinquency receive fullest consideration.

All the aspects of a rational education based on the nature and needs of childhood claim attention here.

The various types of schools, the various methods of teaching particular subjects, the relation between work and play, learning and doing, the school and the community, are discussed for the benefit of parents and teachers.

Another group of volumes deals with special traits of childhood and youth,—their reading and dramatic interests, clothes and personal appearance, the use of money, etc.

The entire series is under the general editorship of Dr. M. V. O'Shea, Professor of Education, University of Wisconsin, and probably the best and widest known authority on educational subjects in America.

Every book in the Childhood and Youth Series is of value to the parent who wishes the best for his child and to the teacher who is seeking higher efficiency.

The Bobbs-Merrill Company
Publishers, Indianapolis

AUTHORS OF BOOKS IN THE

CHILDHOOD AND YOUTH SERIES

FLORENCE HOLBROOK
Principal of the Forestville School, Chicago; author of Round the Year in Myth and Song, Studies in Poetry, Etc.

DAVID STARR JORDAN
Chancellor of Stanford University; author of Care and Culture of Men, Footnotes to Evolution, Etc., Etc.

C. A. McMURRY
Director of Normal Training, Superintendent of Schools, DeKalb, Illinois; author of A Series of General and Special Methods in School Work.

JUNIUS L. MERIAM
Professor of School Supervision, University of Missouri; author of Normal School Education, Etc.

JAMES T. NOE
Professor of Education, University of Kentucky.

RAYMOND RIORDON
Director of the Raymond Riordon School, on Chodikee Lake, N. Y.; author of Lincoln Memorial School—A New Idea in Industrial Education, Etc.

WALTER SARGENT
Professor of Art Education, University of Chicago; author of Fine and Industrial Arts in the Elementary Schools.

FRANK CHAPMAN SHARP
Professor of Philosophy, The University of Wisconsin; author of Shakespeare's Portrayal of the Moral Life, Etc.

ALFRED E. STEARNS
Principal of Phillips Academy, Andover, Mass.; author of various articles in the Atlantic Monthly, Outlook, Etc.

WINTHROP ELLSWORTH STONE
President Purdue University; Member of the Indiana State Board of Education.

THOMAS A. STOREY
Professor of Hygiene, College of the City of New York, Secretary Fourth International Congress on School Hygiene.

M. H. STUART
Principal Manual Training High School, Indianapolis.

BLANCHE M. TRILLING
Director of Women's Gymnasium, The University of Wisconsin.

GUY MONTROSE WHIPPLE
Assistant Professor of Educational Psychology, Cornell University; author of Questions in Psychology, Etc.

The Bobbs-Merrill Company
Publishers, Indianapolis

The Childhood and Youth Series

NATURAL EDUCATION

Mrs. Stoner explains the methods by which she made her daughter "the best developed child in America" mentally, morally and physically; the simple yet astonishing methods which make for the health, happiness and wisdom of any normal child.

By MRS. WINIFRED SACKVILLE STONER
Director-General Women's International Health League

LEARNING BY DOING

The way to learn how to run an automobile is by running it. Professor Swift shows how this practical principle may be applied to history, literature and language-study. A book that breaks up monotony in teaching, stirs enthusiasm, makes the parent and teacher see the child's point of view.

By EDGAR JAMES SWIFT
Professor of Psychology and Education, Washington University; author of Mind in the Making, Etc.

THE CHILD AND HIS SPELLING

Can your child spell? Business and professional men think the children of this generation poor spellers. What's the trouble with the way spelling is taught at home and in school? The authors of this book make a simple but scientific analysis of the whole question.

By WILLIAM A. COOK
Assistant Professor of Education, University of Colorado; and
M. V. O'SHEA
Professor of Education, University of Wisconsin

THE HIGH-SCHOOL AGE

The "teen age" is the critical age, the dangerous age of adolescence, when the future of the child's life is largely determined and the bending of the twig inclines the tree. Professor King here shows parent and teacher how to solve the difficult and all-important problems of this crisis.

By IRVING KING
Professor of Education, University of Iowa; author of Psychology of Child Development, Etc.

Each volume with Special Introduction by the General Editor, M. V. O'Shea, Analytical Table of Contents, Carefully Selected Lists of Books for Reference, Further Reading and Study, and a Full Index.

Each, 12mo, Cloth, One Dollar Net

The Bobbs-Merrill Company
Publishers, Indianapolis

The Childhood and Youth Series

THE WAYWARD CHILD

A practical treatment of the causes of juvenile delinquency and methods of its prevention, by one who has extensive experience in dealing with the young.

By MRS. FREDERIC SCHOFF

President National Congress of Mothers and Parent-Teacher Association; President Philadelphia Juvenile Court and Probation Association; Collaborator, Home Education Division, Bureau of Education

FEAR

A comprehensive, concrete discussion of (1) psychology of fear; (2) varieties of fears found normally in childhood and youth; (3) ways in which fears are expressed and their effects; (4) treatment of fear in home and school.

By G. STANLEY HALL

President Clark University, Worcester, Mass.; author of Adolescence, Educational Problems, Etc.

SELF-HELP

Practical aid to parents and teachers in teaching children to do things for themselves, written by a mother, teacher and keen student of Madame Montessori, Froebel, Pestalozzi, et al.

By DOROTHY CANFIELD FISHER

Author of A Montessori Mother, English Composition of Rhetoric. Etc.

THE USE OF MONEY

How to train the young to appreciate (1) what money represents in labor and privilege; (2) how it may best be expended.

By E. A. KIRKPATRICK

Head of Department of Psychology and Child-Study, State Normal School, Fitchburg, Mass.; author of Fundamentals of Child-Study, The Individual in the Making, Etc.

THE BACKWARD CHILD

A volume dealing with the causes of backwardness among children and also the technique of determining when a child is backward, and practical methods of treating him.

By ARTHUR HOLMES

Dean of the General Faculty, Pennsylvania State College; author of The Conservation of the Child, Etc.

Each Volume With Special Introduction By the General Editor, M. V. O'Shea, Analytical Table of Contents, Carefully Selected Lists of Books for Reference, Further Reading and Study, and a Full Index.

Each, 12mo, Cloth, One Dollar Net

The Bobbs-Merrill Company

Publishers. Indianapolis

THE best-developed child in America, Winifred Sackville Stoner, Jr., could speak several languages and wrote for newspapers and magazines at the age of five, and yet retained all of the characteristics of a healthy, playful child.

At the age of nine she passed the college entrance examinations, and now at twelve, she has mastered eight languages, has written nine books, is a teacher of Esperanto, an accomplished musician, and is stronger physically than the average child of her age.

She is not a GENIUS nor a WONDER CHILD, but simply a NORMAL CHILD WELL DEVELOPED through a system of NATURAL EDUCATION invented by her mother, Mrs. Winifred Sackville Stoner, from whom she has received her training.

Any mother can do for her child what Mrs. Stoner has done for her daughter, if she employs Mrs. Stoner's methods.

Any mother can learn Mrs. Stoner's system from her book, in which she analyzes, outlines and describes her entire plan as carried out during the education of her daughter from the cradle to her tenth year.

Natural Education
By WINIFRED SACKVILLE STONER
Director-General Women's International Health League

is a book which every parent should read and study as one of the first duties of devoted and successful parenthood.

Like all the books in the famous Childhood and Youth Series, Natural Education is provided with a special introduction by the general editor, Dr. M. V. O'Shea, of the Department of Education in the University of Wisconsin, an analytical table of contents, carefully selected lists of books and magazines for reference, further reading and study, and a full index.

12mo, Cloth, One Dollar Net

The Bobbs-Merrill Company
Publishers, Indianapolis

THE "teen age" is the critical age. Boys and girls cause parents and teachers more anxiety between thirteen and twenty than at any other time. That is the period of adolescence—the formative stage, the high-school age, the turning point when futures are moulded.

It is, at the same time, the period at which the boy and the girl are most baffling and difficult to handle; when an ounce of diplomacy can accomplish more with them than a pound of dictum.

As a specialist and an authority, Professor Irving King has prepared a veritable handbook on parental and pedagogical diplomacy which will ease the way of parents and teachers in dealing with children during the formative period and lead to far better results. He devotes special attention to the question of co-education and the question of handling mature, maturing and immature children of the same age. He clears up the problems so confusing to the adult mind and offers helpful suggestions.

The physical changes which take place during the early adolescent age; the intellectual and emotional developments which parallel them; and questions of health and school work as well as practical matters pertaining to the conservation of the energy and efficiency of high-school pupils are given full consideration in

The High-School Age

By IRVING KING
Assistant Professor of Education, University of Iowa; author of Psychology of Child Development, Etc.

No parent or teacher can read this work without feeling a keener appreciation of the vital period in the child's life and without being assisted to a better understanding of how to deal most wisely with the boy or girl who is passing rapidly from childhood to maturity.

THE HIGH-SCHOOL AGE is one of the books in the CHILDHOOD AND YOUTH SERIES, undoubtedly the most important collection of practical educational works for parents and teachers ever produced in this country. As a guide for the home or school it is unexcelled.

12mo, Cloth, One Dollar Net

The Bobbs-Merrill Company
Publishers, Indianapolis

CAN your child spell? Spelling takes more attention in the home than almost any other subject taught in the schools. The drills and practice exercises, the daily preparation for subsequent work in the class-room call for the parent's cooperation.

No subject taught in the schools requires more individual attention than Spelling, on the part of the teacher, who is continually confronted with new problems as to how best the subject may be presented to meet individual differences on the part of pupils.

William A. Cook, Assistant Professor of Education in the University of Colorado, and M. V. O'Shea, Professor of Education in the University of Wisconsin, have conducted a series of investigations extending over a considerable period, with a view to contributing to the solution of the various problems connected with the teaching of spelling.

First, an examination of the spelling history and abilities of a large number of pupils in a rather general way was carried on. Second, a study was made of a small group in a very thorough-going manner. Third, followed an examination of about 300,000 words in common usage, both in speech and correspondence, in order to determine which words should receive attention in the spelling vocabulary.

The Child and His Spelling

By WILLIAM A. COOK and M. V. O'SHEA

contains the results of these experiments, and presents a thoroughgoing, practicable explanation of (1) the psychology of spelling; (2) effective methods of teaching spelling; (3) spelling needs of typical Americans; (4) words pupils should learn.

The material contained in The Child and His Spelling will be found of the greatest value to teachers and to parents who desire to co-operate at home with the work of the school in the education of children. This work constitutes one volume of the CHILDHOOD AND YOUTH SERIES.

12mo, Cloth, One Dollar Net

The Bobbs-Merrill Company
Publishers, Indianapolis

A HUNDRED thousand American mothers venerate the name of Mrs. Frederic Schoff (Hannah Kent Schoff). She has dedicated her life to the work of making the new generation better, stronger and more efficient, and has been an inspiration to every woman in the land to do her full part to insure the future of America.

Through her leadership of the National Congress of Mothers and Parent-Teacher Associations, she is the presiding genius of the greatest educational movement this country has known.

As President of the Philadelphia Juvenile Court and Probation Association, she has had an opportunity to study the wayward children of a great city. She has carried on extensive investigations among men and women confined in prisons and correctional institutions to learn from them at first hand to what they attribute their downfall.

By this broad experience she is qualified to speak with unique authority on the training of children in the home, and especially on the problem of the wayward child.

She makes a forceful appeal to parents both because of their natural desire to guard their children from all harmful influences and because they realize that home training, which comes first of all in every child's life, moulds his morality. If any parent doubts this, he needs more than ever to study

The Wayward Child

By HANNAH KENT SCHOFF

President National Congress of Mothers and Parent-Teacher Associations;
President Philadelphia Juvenile Court and Probation Association

She shows beyond all doubt that the early training in the home can make or unmake characters at will, that homes in which children have been brought up carelessly or inefficiently are largely responsible for the wayward children who later make up our criminal population.

THE WAYWARD CHILD is one of the books in the CHILDHOOD AND YOUTH SERIES, undoubtedly the most important collections of practical educational works for parents and teachers ever produced in this country. As a guide for the home or school it is unexcelled.

12mo, Cloth, One Dollar Net

The Bobbs-Merrill Company

Publishers, Indianapolis

H ONESTY is not an inborn trait. It is not the essential inheritance of children of "good families." It is the delicate product of careful training. A proper regard for *mine* and *thine* is effected by a thousand subtle influences of heredity and environment, home and school and community conditions, physical and mental health.

Experts have subjected the whole question to minute scrutiny and proved that the cultivation of honesty is a matter of personal application to the individual child. They have laid the foundation for an entire new "Science of Conduct."

Dr. Healy, Director of the Juvenile Psychopathic Institute and adviser to the Juvenile Court in Chicago, is one of these experts. He gives the parent, teacher and social worker the benefit of broad, sane, sound observation.

The quickest way to a cure for stealing, Dr. Healy believes, is to find the way to the inner mental life of the delinquent, and he reveals how this may be accomplished in

Honesty
By WILLIAM HEALY

His aim is to prevent and to cure stealing by children. By the faithful description of many actual cases of theft, their underlying causes and successful or bungling treatment, he shows what to guard against and what to foster; how to make a proper diagnosis and effect the cure. He writes with tolerance, sympathy, kindliness, for he loves children.

THE CHILDHOOD AND YOUTH SERIES, in which HONESTY is issued, includes works on the special traits of childhood, as well as books dealing with various phases in the physical, mental, moral and social development of the child.

12mo, Cloth, One Dollar Net

The Bobbs-Merrill Company
Publishers, Indianapolis

THE civilized world is awakening to the rights
of the child, and to the fact that its right of
rights is the right to be well-born. Heredity is
recognized as a factor of supreme importance in
determining the child's nature; yet there is no
subject on which there is such general ignorance
and so much superstition.

What is "prenatal influence," and what are its limitations?
What traits and habits may be transmitted? How far does the
parent's body and brain and character affect the child's heritage
at birth, and how far the more remote ancestor's? Do degenerate parents beget degenerate children? To what extent are
physical and mental defects due to inheritance and not to environment or training?

On these and similar questions there is the widest
difference of opinion and belief, and the grossest error,
among intelligent people who are not familiar with the
latest results of scientific study.

Professor Guyer, of the University of Wisconsin, who has
studied the whole problem of heredity in a thoroughgoing way,
has prepared a book to take away the mystery and misunderstanding, and to enlighten parents, teachers and social workers
on an all-important subject. He calls it

Being Well-Born

By MICHAEL F. GUYER
Professor of Zoology in the University of Wisconsin,
Author of Animal Micrology, etc.

His work includes an account of the new science of Eugenics
which is striving for the betterment of the race, the conservation
of good stock and the repression of bad.

This concrete, practical book on Heredity and Eugenics
naturally falls in THE CHILDHOOD AND YOUTH
SERIES, which undertakes to treat child-nature from
every viewpoint, and which is the most complete, scientific and satisfactory collection of books on child-problems
now published.

12mo, Cloth, One Dollar Net

The Bobbs-Merrill Company
Publishers, Indianapolis

GET in tune with childhood. Take the children's point of view. Find how work and play may be united in their lives in happiest and most effectual combination. See how the monotony of the daily "grind" may be broken and lively, wholesome, compelling interest be aroused in home study, school work and tasks of the day.

Successful learning depends on successful teaching. The romantic spirit of youth revolts against constraint, and the teacher, be he parent or pedagogue, can succeed in educating the child only by establishing between himself and his pupil, the proper sympathetic relation.

Edgar James Swift, Professor of Psychology and Education, Washington University, St. Louis, after years of extended experiment, has learned ways and means of accomplishing this and has collected a vast amount of valuable information concerning methods of turning to educational advantage the adventurous overflow of youthful energy.

He shows how home and school studies may take on a vital relation to the actual daily life of children and how enthusiasm for their work may be inculcated in the young. All this is told, in a manner to quicken the interest of parents and teachers, in

Learning by Doing

By EDGAR JAMES SWIFT
Author of Mind in the Making, Etc.

Make the child as happy in his work as he is in his play by finding how you can appeal to his individual interests, tendencies and intellectual traits, and how the learner may be taught with the least resistance and greatest efficiency.

This is precisely the book for every parent and teacher who wants to make study a pastime and not a drudgery. It is included in the CHILDHOOD AND YOUTH SERIES, the important new collection of books for parents and teachers.

12mo, Cloth, One Dollar Net

The Bobbs-Merrill Company
Publishers, Indianapolis

CPSIA information can be obtained
at www.ICGtesting.com
Printed in the USA
BVHW072339250620
582143BV00004B/417